Relinquishing My Dreams

Relinquishing *My* Dreams
How to Survive a Prodigal

SUE BURROWS AND TRICIA BRADLEY

ADELPHE COMMUNICATIONS LLC
FISHERS, INDIANA

Cover Design: Dan Elkins, LIFT Ministries
Interior Design/Cover Completion: Donya Dunlap

ISBN: 978-0-9820444-0-7

10 9 8 7 6 5 4 3 2 1

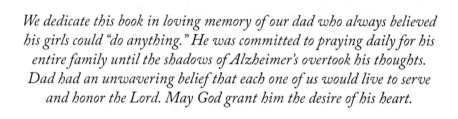

We dedicate this book in loving memory of our dad who always believed his girls could "do anything." He was committed to praying daily for his entire family until the shadows of Alzheimer's overtook his thoughts. Dad had an unwavering belief that each one of us would live to serve and honor the Lord. May God grant him the desire of his heart.

Acknowledgements

A project of this magnitude involves the hands and hearts of many people. To all of you who worked alongside me, I say thank you for your labor of love. I also deeply appreciate those of you who were prayer warriors on my behalf; your prayers sustained me through the worst of times.

Thank you to Pastor Craig Scott whose sermon at The Wilds inspired me to consider writing this book. I appreciate your enthusiasm for truth and your willingness to encourage a novice.

To Michael Hoover, you are valued more than you will ever know. Your commitment to "excellence in the details" is evident on every inch of this manuscript. Your serene spirit kept me calm in hectic moments and your generosity inspired me to keep going. Thank you for pouring your life into this book and for sharing my burden for this ministry. May God richly reward you.

Lauri, you are a terrific author's assistant! Your expertise pointed me to a team of people whom God used to finish this project in a timely fashion. The final product exceeds my expectations and is far more polished than I could have accomplished on my own.

I am also indebted to a small group of precious ladies—Janet, Leanne, Pam, and Suzy—who faithfully met for a year to work through the Bible Studies. A huge hug to each of you! Your input, insight, and support were invaluable; you blessed me often and enriched my life.

This book would never have been possible without my sister, Sue. You have been available to me, particularly the last six years so that I could bare my heart. Every time we talked, you gave me spiritual perspective to lift me out of despair, to look to Jesus to see how He might be working, and to encourage me to offer unconditional love when at times it was very difficult to give. You shared verses of Scripture for me to stand on when all seemed hopeless. You made me giggle and laugh amid the tears. You encouraged me to "turn my misery into a ministry" to women who might be walking a similar road. You persuaded me to take a new approach to the Word of God by getting "inside the skin" of the Bible Characters chosen for this book. I'm grateful you reminded me again and again that God uses ALL types of people and situations. Thank you, Sue, for helping me organize my thoughts, for helping me write this book, for being there, and for being the very best sister in the whole world!

My family is an extraordinary gift from God, and I love each one of you dearly. Steven, thank you for being a pillar of strength, unwavering in your faith. Your integrity and unassuming spirit have been a great example to many people, especially to me. To my children— I'm glad that I'm your Mom! Each of you has taught me valuable lessons, and I'm trusting God that our experience together these last few years will strengthen and bond us for life! You are young people of such promise! My prayer is that each of you would have a heart after God and follow the example of Jesus in everything you do.

To Kirsten, my daughter, an exceptionally special thank you! Not everyone would be so willing to share such a story. My prayer is that others will benefit from our experience and will see how God deals with sin while loving us beyond our imagination.

Above all, I would like to thank the Lord Jesus for walking with me, loving me, and helping me when I literally didn't think I could go on. His leading in my life enabled me to become more transparent and to be willing to share such a personal story. It was only as I walked my own meandering path that God worked in my heart and gave me a compassion for others who were also walking a painful journey.

To God be the glory!

        ॐ Tricia Bradley

Contents

Part One: The Journey

Contents

Part Two: Bible Studies

Contents

A Word from the Author

This book was born out of adversity in the midst of a situation I never imagined would happen to me! Along the way, I met many people who were living with similar circumstances but who had few resources to deal with the pain. I trust God will use this book to support you if you've experienced your own ordeal of betrayal, rejection, isolation, or hopelessness.

There are five distinct components:

- The Narrative of my life with a prodigal
- A Reflection at the end of each chapter highlighting some insights I learned
- A Survival Tip or "battle strategy" at the end of each chapter to help you endure the difficult times
- A series of Lessons based on People of Scripture who faced surprisingly similar circumstances
- A Compilation of Bible verses that became my lifeline on dark days

No one understands the depths of despair like someone who has walked his own path of despair. I have offered my story as an EARTHLY EXAMPLE of the power of God to change an absolutely impossible situation. As I was tempted to look ahead, the future seemed most uncertain, but I was viewing it from a human perspective. Too often, I had forgotten to factor in the power of God Who is able to move the most stubborn "mountain."

More importantly, the Lord impressed upon me to offer you HEAVENLY HOPE, and that can only be found in the pages of God's Word. Nothing anywhere gave me comfort like the promises found in Scripture. These verses renewed my heart and encouraged me throughout my journey. Moreover, they continue to minister to me today.

Even better than merely reading verses, I hope you'll study some of the lives of the people of the Bible and note how God works. He has filled Scripture with the stories of many people that serve as excellent examples for us today. The set of lessons is not a fill-in-the-blank experience. Many questions are open-ended and are designed

────── *A Word from the Author* ──────

to be studied with a few like-minded friends. My prayer is that your heart will be encouraged and your burden lifted as the Holy Spirit teaches you anew about the ways of our Lord.

To be honest, sharing such a personal story publicly is not easy for me. However, I'm convinced God allowed me to walk such a path in order to bring comfort to others who have been similarly devastated.

(Note: Names have been changed in order to offer family and friends some measure of protection.)

୭

Introduction

When I was a little girl, I often dreamed about the future. It was easy to imagine—college graduation, a perfect wedding, a handsome prince, a well-decorated home, and the addition of beautiful children. Never once did I envision hardships along the way. My little dream world changed when Steven and I married and learned that conceiving children was not an "inalienable right." My hopes of having my very own baby were frustrated and then completely dashed.

My husband and I eventually decided to adopt and were delighted when three precious children were placed in our home. Once again my visions of an idyllic family life soared. All went well for a time; then unexpectedly, problems began surfacing with our oldest child. I was stunned when she ran away from home.

I was completely unprepared for life with a prodigal, and there was a lot of pain and uncertainty I had to face. Through it all, the Lord was my Strength, my Guide, and my constant Companion. The fact that I survived this trauma and reemerged with new hope is because of God's grace and unconditional love for me! In addition, the Lord gave me friends who encouraged me on my worst days.

For you who are suddenly faced with a detour in your "perfect life," I offer my journey as an example of the power of God to work in impossible circumstances. May God bless you as you relinquish your own dreams and as you learn to trust Jesus in a deeper way. May He shed light on your path and offer healing for your wounded heart.

&

Part One

&

The Journey

Chapter One

♋

Barrenness

The desert has a beauty all its own, and if a person is prepared to spend time there, it is a source of wonderful treasures. If you, however, are expecting majestic mountains, a breathtaking waterfall, or a lush tropical hideaway, waking up in the Sahara is quite a shock!

That's the best way to describe what it was like to discover my barrenness. At the time, I saw it only as an ugly word that described my disappointment and broken heart. I felt dried-up, left out, and miserable—any oasis of hope evaporated. Like grains of sand irritating every nook and cranny of a child's body, my infertility reared its head all too often. Women reliving labor experiences and sharing parenting stories, the arrival of birth announcements or baby shower invitations, or even sermons on the joys and blessings of Motherhood could send me into a tailspin. While I never encountered someone who deliberately mocked my empty nest, my wounded heart was on my sleeve, and too often I avoided people if I thought they would ask that dreaded question, "Do YOU plan to have any children?"

Steven and I investigated several infertility "solutions," but after considering all the factors, we decided to put our efforts and money into the process of adoption, which turned out to be a formidable course of action. There were a myriad of interviews, a total invasion of privacy, and countless pages of questions. In addition, we were astounded at the financial commitment. Once we submitted all our paper work, we were placed on what seemed like an unending waiting list.

Days turned into weeks and weeks into months, yet there was no change in my situation. I was reminded, however, that I was not alone. The Biblical accounts of Hannah, Elizabeth, Rachel, and Sarah suddenly made much more sense, and now I truly felt their pain.

I even discovered a few dear women who surfaced surprisingly close to me who also struggled with barrenness. I became friends with Mary whose husband worked with mine. She already had a child but was unable to conceive again. We shed many tears as we prayed together and asked for divine intervention. One fall day, Mary had an unmistakable glow on her face; before she said a word, I knew in my heart she was pregnant. I have to admit, I cried a lot that day; I was happy for her and sad for me. It felt like God was listening to her requests and ignoring mine.

She and I continued to meet together and pray. Eventually, I received the call that there was a little girl waiting for us to adopt. GOD HAD INDEED HEARD OUR PRAYERS AND ANSWERED AT LAST! Mary later confided that she prayed specifically that our child would arrive before hers. Kirsten was born on January 31, and Mary's new son was born exactly two months later.

During my years of barrenness, I sobbed many tears and thought many desperate thoughts—like "would I EVER be able to hold my own baby in my arms?" Simply put, the answer was YES! Finally this trip to the desert was about to end, and I came away from it changed. In that place, I met others who understood my agony and some who wept beside me. I developed a tenderness toward hurting people, and God was showing me He works in ways far different than I ever would have imagined. There would be other lessons to learn as well.

℘

Reflection

Looking back I realize what seemed like a dead-end then, was actually an opportunity for God to work in ways I did not foresee. Never underestimate the creativity and power of God!

&

Survival Tip

Remember when the events of life look hopeless to you, they aren't to God.

&

Suggested Bible Study Characters

Hannah

Jacob

Mary Magdalene

&

Chapter Two

&

New Parents

I'll never forget that day—February 5, 1986. I got up, ate breakfast, got dressed—just like on any other morning. This, however, was to be no ordinary day. This day would change my life forever. God would not thunder out of the heavens. He would not send a shaggy-haired prophet to my front door. No, He would use a phone call to change my life forever.

I was seated beside my organ teacher playing and "lifting the rafters" in a cavernous church. I was concentrating on my pedal work and therefore hardly noticed a man handing a note to my very proper and stately instructor. After a quick glance, my teacher casually mentioned I should call home immediately, but he didn't bother to stop teaching. My mind came to life, and various thoughts flooded in—all of them tragic or depressing. Obviously I was worthless at the keyboard; so I calmed my racing heart and shyly asked for a break.

My little shoes clicked down the center aisle of the church, and I thought I would never reach the phone. It didn't even occur to me that this could be BABY news. After all, the last time I checked, the adoption agency had no expectant mothers available. Even worse, we were told that in the last year, only about 25 babies had been placed. With well over 1,000 couples waiting, it didn't look promising for us to receive a baby anytime soon.

My fingers trembled as I called home. Steven answered and said, "We just got a call, and there is a baby girl waiting for us!" The noise I let out was infinitely louder than the music I had just finished.

I was ecstatic and delirious with joy! Just then, my unemotional teacher came into the office to find out what all the commotion was about. Out of character for him, he put his arm on my shoulder and carefully asked if there was anything he could do for me.

I blurted out, "I JUST BECAME A MOTHER!" All he could ask was, "During your organ lesson?" The answer of course was YES!

෨

Reflection

Looking back my heart still warms and my face still glows as I recall this day. Isn't it wonderful that God gives us good memories to relive later when the road is uncertain?

℘

Survival Tip

Make every effort to maintain focus on the true, honest, pure, and lovely aspects of your life—past and present. (Philippians 4:8) Satan would love to drag you down in despair and discouragement; so fight back with a heavenly perspective.

℘

Suggested Bible Study Characters

Elijah

Elisha

℘

Chapter Three

❦

Expectations

*T*hat phone call sent me into a flurry of activity. I raced home and gathered the small stash of items I'd collected in the event we would receive a baby. Now finally, Steven and I were about to become parents...HALLELUJAH! We chatted continually for the three-hour trip and settled on the name Kirsten Janae, meaning "the Peace of Christ."

We tried very hard to compose ourselves when we walked up to the front door of the adoption agency. As we waited rather impatiently, the director droned on and on about the papers we needed to sign and the legalities that awaited us. We could hear a baby crying in the next room, and the only thing I wanted to do was to get my hands on my daughter.

That first moment was incredible, and I still get goose bumps as I relive it. I remember looking into Kirsten's little blue eyes and being convinced she was the most gorgeous and precious baby ever created. Our fondest hopes had come true at last.

The next three years sped by in a whirlwind of activity as we welcomed two more equally special babies into our home. Steven and I believed then (and still do) that out of all the possibilities in the world, God specifically and personally selected us to be the parents of these three endearing children. We could not have loved them more.

We began our adventure of parenthood with great passion and set happily and intentionally about our task. Above all, we wanted our children to know the Lord Jesus, trust Him as their Savior, and follow His leading for their lives. We wanted them to be people of integrity. We wanted to give them plenty of opportunities to love beautiful music and to enjoy sports. Our desire was that they would be free to pursue the academic path of God's choosing. Simply put, we wanted to be full-time parents who loved their children well.

Diapers, crayons, and toy trucks interrupted our simple and serene lives. Steven often commented that when a person waits six long years to have children, sleepless nights or spit-up on your clothes is a small price to pay.

From the beginning Kirsten had a strong will, but her mounds of blonde curls and precocious ways charmed everyone she met. We spent a lot of time learning Bible verses. The first one she quoted was Genesis 1:1, but in her language she blurted out "Jennifer's 1:1: In the beginning God cwee-ated the heaven and the earth." She loved telling the story about Adam and his wife, "Even."

We not only adopted her, but our extended family and a gazillion church friends also adopted her. Everyone loved her, and we proudly showed her off whenever we could. Looking back on that sweet time, we remember eagerly anticipating what God might possibly do with such a girl.

Elementary school days were busy and filled with books, flute lessons, church activities, and normal chaos. My sister warned me about the possibility of an independent and rebellious spirit sneaking in during the junior high years, but I naively dismissed her words. From what I knew, Kirsten was a happy, well-adjusted, hard-working pre-teen. While we did face a few disciplinary challenges, nothing seemed out of the ordinary.

Flowers were blooming, the sun was shining, stars were bright, and all was well. We did not notice the dark clouds forming or the approaching storm. Little did we know we were in for some uncertain times ahead.

ॐ

Reflection

Looking back I realize how sweet this time was as we bonded with our children and made every effort, we thought, to prepare them for the future. What we didn't know then, is how different that future would turn out to be.

৪০

Survival Tip

Enjoy each day you have with your children, and diligently impart spiritual truth to them. Deliberately commit them into the hands of the Lord and know that He will walk with you both now and in the future.

৪০

Suggested Bible Study Characters

Cain

Mary

৪০

Chapter Four

❧

Turbulent Times

As we walked through the teen years, we started to feel uneasy. Something wasn't quite right with Kirsten. However, she was our first child, and we didn't exactly know what was "typical" adolescent behavior.

As time passed, however, we became increasingly concerned about her preoccupation with certain friends and boys. She was fixated on their approval and affection. As we started monitoring her more closely, our fears were confirmed. She was writing and receiving inappropriate notes and had even gone off with a couple of different boys between youth group activities and church.

Because we took our responsibility as parents seriously, we tried to limit outside influences and attempted to instill Christian principles. We thought we had been consistent, open and honest, but she was retreating into a place beyond our grasp. We hoped for a quick recovery, but God had many lessons for us all to learn. We second-guessed ourselves and asked lots of questions.

- Is this just a phase she's going through?
- Is she hiding something?
- Is someone encouraging her to make poor choices?
- What is she really thinking?
- Is she bothered by her adoption?
- Is she telling us the truth?
- Are we too harsh, or are we too lenient?
- Is something wrong, or are we being paranoid?

We talked, we cried, we phoned family and friends, we worried, we fretted, we sought counsel, we clung to Scripture, and we read books; but most of all, we prayed. As time went on, we came to the conclusion that Kirsten had some very serious issues to deal with, and what was happening went beyond normal adolescent struggles.

It's a good thing that we had a deep-seated faith in God's Word because our sweet little journey of parenthood turned terribly frightening. One moment we were blissfully enjoying the road of life, and then all too soon we found ourselves being sucked down a sinkhole of lies and deceit without an end in sight.

Steven was on staff at a large church in the Midwest, and we were accustomed to people turning to us for help. Now, however, we were the ones with a problem, and humanly speaking, we didn't know where to turn. We felt alone, despairing, and emotionally bruised.

It was easy and natural for us to take our concerns to the Lord in prayer, but it was much harder for us to share our heavy hearts with others. We did not want to embarrass Kirsten by sharing all the details, and we didn't know how people would react to her "indiscretions" or our inability to handle her. Our relationship with her was already strained, and we didn't want to make the situation worse. In addition, we naively reasoned all would be fine rather quickly; so why should we inform others of our plight? As we looked around at our friends, we thought no one else had children in crisis; we mistakenly assumed we were the only ones dealing with such an ordeal.

To make matters worse, I grew up believing that people really didn't want to hear about all your problems. So I tended to put a smile on my face—no matter what. It was relatively easy to say, "Everything is fine; I'm okay," but in reality, few aspects of our life were fine. I was too proud or too ashamed to openly share that we had a problem in our home. Looking back now, I believe Satan wanted us to be quiet; and, therefore, we became isolated from the very ones who would love us best and would encourage us to trust God.

God works in the most unusual ways and with the most unlikely people. (If you don't believe me, study the characters of the Bible or the heroes of church history.) To us, these were uncertain times, but the Lord was working in our lives in ways we never would have imagined before. He was pushing us out of our comfort zone and giving us new hearts BECAUSE of the misery we were enduring. Only God would think of turning a weakness into strength and a problem into a ministry.

∞

Reflection

Looking back it seems so foolish to think we could make it through a parenting crisis without leaning on our Christian friends. I've since discovered the benefits of meeting regularly with a few women in similar circumstances. As Solomon says in Ecclesiastes 4:9-10, "Two are better than one, because they have a good return for their work: If one falls down, his friend can help him up."

❧

Survival Tip

Any load is lighter if it's shared; so by all means, find someone who will listen to your heart, support you in prayer, and give you spiritual perspective. Satan wants to defeat you in this battle; he wants you to face him naked and alone.

❧

Suggested Bible Study Characters

David

Elijah

❧

Chapter Five

🙰

Expelled from School

Our first experience with parenthood was not turning out to be like we expected. Instead of smooth sailing, our journey continued to be increasingly stormy. Each time we thought, "at least things can't get much worse," it seems like they did.

It all started with Kirsten telling "little" lies. Then we noticed odd bits of behavior as she became secretive about her friends and her room. We were more troubled as we began to receive phone calls from school and comments from our neighbors. She became increasingly defiant of well-known family standards.

We were saddened as we watched her personality disintegrate. Just a few years before, she had been a friendly, tenderhearted child who brought sunshine and joy wherever she went. Now she was more brooding and self-conscious. She seemed to be obsessed with the approval of others and wanted a boyfriend very badly. We had long conversations with her and were even more concerned as we listened to her perspective. To complicate matters, Kirsten had many questions regarding her adoption. Our initial assessment was that our daughter was upset with God and living in a dream world.

We did NOT want to become overly suspicious, "private-investigator" parents, and so we prayed earnestly that whenever she would be involved in something rebellious, we would find out. Indeed, her sins would come to light in the most unbelievable ways and through the most amazing circumstances.

Our life at home began to follow this pattern:
- We'd uncover a problem.
- We'd confront Kirsten.
- She'd deny it in anger.
- She'd cry.
- She'd apologize.
- Then we'd start over again.

Our once peaceful home was now filled with constant tension, many suspicions, and lots of "missiles" launched about. Everyone was in pain. How far we were living from the hopes and dreams we held just a few years earlier.

Kirsten attended a conservative Christian school and had developed the ability to circumvent the rules. It didn't take us long to figure out that an emphasis on outward conformity does not always impact the heart.

Unlike at a public high school where expulsions are reserved for serious offenses like weapons, drugs, or assaults, her school had different expectations and standards. Demerits were also given for transgressions such as late homework, tardies, unsuitable language, and rowdy behavior. As punishments accumulated, it was possible for students to be expelled for a series of relatively minor offenses.

One day we received a call from the principal; Kirsten was about to be expelled for writing a series of inappropriate notes. We were alarmed and dismayed; this was proof that her situation was serious and that there would be far-reaching consequences. At a small Christian school, bad news travels fast, especially if it concerns the child of a minister. In addition, it was quite a shock to those who had been unaware of our plight, particularly Kirsten's beloved grandfather who was just entering the twilight years of Alzheimer's.

Our hopes were shattered, and any pride we had vanished. Steven felt if he couldn't even lead his own daughter to godliness, he had no business being a pastor. He was prepared to resign, but our senior pastor strongly discouraged it. He believed disqualification for ministry was appropriate only when parents failed to address the issues of their children.

We had always assumed Kirsten would go to college. She scored "off the charts" on all standardized testing, and we had no doubts she would be successful academically. We had even envisioned her with a graduate degree in science or computer arts. Now what were we to do? We considered many possibilities and finally decided to home-educate her. We knew this decision would present its own set of difficulties, but we felt the benefits outweighed any negatives. Kirsten, bent on getting her own way and dependent on certain friendships, was NOT happy at all.

We didn't know it at the time, but the next year would bring even more pain and a sense of hopelessness to us all. We wondered… Would we EVER be joyful again? Would we EVER get out of this horrendous pit?

❧

Reflection

Looking back I remember how frustrated I was trying to help a child so determined to go her own way. I believed if I could just say the right word or find the right motivation, Kirsten would come back to us. I soon learned that some children are so stubborn and determined that few things will break their will until they begin to reap the consequences of their actions.

ଐ

Survival Tip

Consequences of sin can be very hurtful, and moms sometimes rush in too soon to save a child from pain. Don't be too quick to relieve the negative effects of wrongdoing. Allow God to work BECAUSE OF the pain. (Hebrews 12:5-11)

ଐ

Suggested Bible Study Characters

David

Job

Joseph

Samson

ଐ

Chapter Six

&

Five Surprises

*I*t had been a very hard year for all of us. Kirsten felt she was always in trouble and couldn't do anything right; what she didn't realize was that we were struggling too. All of us were in agony; our relationship with Kirsten was spinning out of control, and there seemed to be no relief.

We tried everything. We talked about issues; we tiptoed around them. We tried punishment; we tried praise. We withheld privileges; we offered rewards. We limited certain friendships; we encouraged others. Through it all, we had a few victories, but our family life was really suffering.

Home-educating Kirsten was quite difficult. By nature, she was a gregarious, self-reliant social butterfly; so being stuck at home 24 hours a day was simply intolerable. She believed she had no friends and no fun. She was confined to one house with 2 brothers and 2 parents who were "2 strict." It didn't take us long to figure out if "Kirsten ain't happy, nobody's happy!"

We tried to imagine life through her eyes, and we attempted to figure out the root cause of her rebellion. Was it her adoption? Did she feel like she was not a full-blown member of our family? Did she think our love was too small to forgive her? Had she given up all hope of reconciling with us? Truthfully, the root cause of her rebellion was a sinful heart and an estranged relationship with God. It is no exaggeration to say Kirsten was in the middle of a gigantic spiritual battle for her soul.

Kirsten's 16th birthday was approaching, and we decided to

throw her an unforgettable party to demonstrate unequivocally our commitment and love for her. We promised five surprises to be revealed over the course of the next week and knew her curiosity about them would help her look ahead with joy.

Since her birth month is January, we concentrated on the message of "fresh starts." The New Year is an obvious time to wipe the slate clean and commemorate God's forgiveness that makes us all "white as snow." We were excited as we happily planned and plotted the fun.

Surprise #1 came in the form of my sister who flew across the country from California. We sneaked her down the stairs and into a packing box in the basement. We brought Kirsten down and could almost hear her heart beat as she heard strange noises behind her. Then her wild and crazy aunt suddenly emerged and scared a delighted Kirsten half to death!

Surprise #2 was sitting outside our home the next evening. We led her to believe we were making a pizza run for just our family—but it was to be much more. As we stepped out the front door, Kirsten was rendered speechless to see a brand-new canary yellow Mustang sitting in our driveway. Her dad told her it was borrowed for her enjoyment that night and she could drive it herself in the church parking lot as long as he was her co-pilot. I don't know which one had the bigger smile as they took off down the street.

Surprise #3 was a party of about 12 girls waiting at a friend's house. Kirsten and Steven drove out in the country and laughed out loud in pure joy. That night, our daughter had a new view of her dad as the coolest parent in the world. Kirsten said, "Let's drive by Erica's house to show off this car." Unbeknownst to Kirsten, that was the very place of the party. Can you imagine the shock on Kirsten's face when she knocked on the door and all her friends spilled out yelling, "SURPRISE!!!"

Those girls made a lot of noise and ate a lot of food. I sat back and watched my daughter enjoy a whole group of friends and look happier than I'd seen her in weeks. She received many thoughtful gifts, and laughter filled the room. Hopefully this would be a turning point for her, and Kirsten would fully comprehend that she was well-loved by many people.

Surprise #4 was a special gift she opened that night from her grandparents in California. It was a gold rope chain that symbolized a prayer promise from them to her. Ecclesiastes 4:12b says, "A cord of three strands is not quickly broken." They wanted her to know that every time she looked at it, that they were praying for her to make right choices and to realize she was not alone in her struggle. It was easy to see that Kirsten's heart was touched as she read their card.

Surprise #5 was the last one of the evening and perhaps the best. The girls became quiet as Steven started to talk. He choked up as he pulled out a beautiful ring we had carefully selected for her. It contained five diamonds that signified each member of our family. The gems were nestled closely together, just like our desire for our family to stick together. There was a filigree of S's that wound around the ring; we wanted them to serve as a reminder of the Savior Who would offer hope and help every time she needed Him. We LOVED our daughter, and that was the message we wanted to clearly communicate to her. We didn't have a million impossible rules for her to live by. We wanted her to live her life governed by purity and honesty, and so we engraved those words inside her ring. Steven finished by praying a wonderful blessing over her; I don't think there was a dry eye in the place.

It seemed that Kirsten was more tender as we drove home that night. We were delirious with joy because we believed this night was indeed the beginning of a fresh start for her. Hopefully, she finally realized how very much we loved her. Maybe now we could end this difficult time in her life and move on to bigger and better things.

℃

Reflection

Looking back I have no regrets for all the love we specifically planned into this evening. Our goal was to make an indelible imprint on her heart that NO MATTER WHAT, WE LOVED OUR DAUGHTER! In the years since this event, Kirsten has continually said, "I never doubted you loved me."

৫০

Survival Tip

Find ways to express your unconditional love for your child—in word or in deed, with gifts or with kindness, in reproof or in mercy. You'll NEVER regret the effort or cost to you personally. If Jesus could die for us "while we were still sinners," then it's possible for us to communicate our love to wayward children. (Romans 5:8)

৫০

Suggested Bible Study Characters

Jonah

The Prodigal

The Woman Taken in Adultery

৫০

Chapter Seven

&

Enter Christopher

I've watched new moms holding their infants and gazing on them with great pride and wonder. I've watched dads cheering for their little kids playing soccer with the enthusiasm of World Cup fans. I've heard parents musing about the future for their children and beaming over all the possibilities awaiting them. We, too, were no different; we were grateful for the opportunity to be parents three-times over, and we could easily see great potential for each one of our children.

When Kirsten was young, she wanted to be a cowboy, and knowing her unrelenting determination, we wondered if that would be a reality. As she grew older, we were pleased about the variety of areas in which she excelled. She played the flute beautifully; she loved science and anything related to a computer. She was athletic and competed well in Bible quizzing and speech. Her future looked bright academically.

We also wondered about the man she might marry. Kirsten was a most determined girl. She was organized, opinionated, and extremely industrious. Her future husband would have to be unique and wonderful, and of course, a fine Christian. We looked ahead to the time we would actually meet her Prince Charming, and like all parents, wistfully imagined her wedding day and her "happily ever after."

We prayed for years for our yet-unknown son-in-law. When we finally met him, we were surprised to hear that his name was

Christopher which literally means "Christ bearer." He was so different from the type of person we expected to pair with our daughter. I guess we overlooked how often God puts together opposites in marriage. (When I stop to think about it, Steven and I came from different regions of the country, and our formative years were spent in decidedly different circumstances. In addition, our paths took some amazing detours on our way to the altar, and we're still married!) Nevertheless, the circumstances surrounding our introduction to Christopher were less than ideal. Kirsten's initial mention of him was couched in a lie, and the relationship among us began going downhill.

Before long, we discovered that Kirsten and Christopher were corresponding without our permission and were secretly meeting after we had retired for the night. Christopher believed he was protecting Kirsten from an undesirable home situation; we believed he was encouraging her dishonesty and rebellion. Kirsten believed we wouldn't give her a chance to date him; we believed we were making the right choice based on what we knew at the time. Turmoil and suspicion began to dominate life at home.

After much prayer, we felt it was our duty to erect some boundaries hoping we could prevent Kirsten from possibly ruining her future. We tried to assert more control, thinking we could change her heart. Instead she felt smothered and used every opportunity to go around, under, over, and through our protective walls. This was a frightening chapter in our parenting saga, and we were shaken deeply.

She soon made it clear that our standards of dress, friends, music, and money were no longer governing her life. We were devastated and bewildered. Our main question was, "Why would a girl with such promise reject everything she had been taught?"

At the time, it was tempting to blame Christopher for Kirsten's unrest, but we knew even then, this perspective was not a fair or accurate assessment. We all were struggling with issues we didn't even know existed, and our response was not always calm or productive.

This was a difficult time for all of us, and it would be a long time before our family would begin to heal.

❧

Reflection

Looking back I have a new appreciation for the mysterious workings of God. For many reasons, we had a difficult time loving Christopher in the beginning. He, however, accepted Jesus as His Savior, and we faithfully pray that he will be a good role model for our grandson. In the darkest of circumstances, we never dreamed we would ever have a good relationship, but we continue to enjoy a sweet connection with him even to this day. Who would have thought such an event possible? God would!

∞

Survival Tip

If you speak disparaging comments about your child's friends (no matter how truthful your remarks might be), he may become defensive and closed to anything you will ever say. As difficult as it may seem, look at the acquaintances of your prodigal with the heart of Jesus. You never know which one of them might possibly become a member of your own family.

∞

Suggested Bible Study Characters

Jacob

Peter

The Prodigal Son

The Woman Taken in Adultery

∞

Chapter Eight

&

Matters of the Heart

Anyone knows that heart problems aren't to be taken lightly; they can be scary and deadly. In our case, we had known for years that Steven would eventually face open-heart surgery. The good news was that his heart could be fixed—but not until the capacity of his aortic valve had diminished significantly.

He never had any symptoms of his condition until just before his 54th birthday. Then he began experiencing a rapid heartbeat (200+ beats per minute) and shortness of breath, both of which left my ex-Marine husband exhausted and nearly incapacitated. His cardiologist set the date for a diagnostic test to be followed by valve replacement surgery.

I have to admit I was concerned especially after listening to all the complications that might occur. This was serious! On the day of his test, I went to the health club to work out, and as I trudged away on the treadmill, I remember praying a lot—committing my husband, my sons, and my daughter to the Lord.

On the way out, the receptionist stopped me and said, "Tricia, your husband just phoned us. Please call home right away. It is a family emergency." EMERGENCY??? My mind immediately went into overdrive.

- Was Steven in a car accident?
- Was he having a problem with his heart?
- Did something happen to my dad with Alzheimer's?
- Did someone in the church family have a crisis?

When I finally got the news, it was beyond what I had imagined.

Steven simply said, "Tricia, I found a note on Kirsten's bed. She has run away from home." Later we were to learn that she was with Christopher.

I could not believe it, and my mind raced with lots of questions. How could she do such a thing? Where would she feel safer than in our home? Why didn't she talk to us? Were there others who were influencing her? What kind of trouble was she in that would provoke such a drastic step?

After I caught my breath, I got very angry. Of all times to rebel in such a dramatic way, this girl chose a vulnerable time, perhaps even a fatal time for her dad! Was this a cry for help, or was she just being foolish and selfish? I vacillated between being sick with grief and wanting to "strangle her" with my own two hands. There was no doubt that we loved our daughter deeply, but nothing seemed to be going right in our relationship.

So we entered a new and more troubling stage in our life with Kirsten. We asked ourselves two questions over and over:
- How do we fix HER rebellious heart?
- Where do we go to fix OUR own broken hearts?

We came to the conclusion that there was no surgeon on earth or operation known to man that could heal our pain. Our faith would be sorely tested over the next several months as we begged Heaven for answers and cried out for relief.

When I finally made it home, Steven and I went into immediate action. We called everyone we knew, but we couldn't find Kirsten. She was only 16, and we were devastated as nightfall approached. We prayed for God to watch over her, protect her, and bring her back to us. I was fearful that Steven's physical heart couldn't take it, but he often said, "I would gladly give my life for Kirsten. If my death would bring her back to the Lord and to us, it would be worth it."

We wearily went to the hospital the next morning for Steven's heart catheterization. During the procedure, I checked my phone messages over and over again hoping for word from her, but there were none. Then, just as Steven was coming out of recovery, I looked up, and to my surprise, Kirsten walked in! I could hardly contain myself as I hugged her and cried for joy that she had returned.

This would not be the happy ending for which I had hoped. The first words out of her mouth were, "Mom, we need to talk. I want to grow up." Would we survive this new turn of events?

🙰

Reflection

Looking back I still feel the agony of this day, but I've learned a valuable lesson from it—a broken heart forces the patient to seek help, make changes, and perhaps undergo surgery. Just as Steven's pain sent us to a doctor, the pain of a broken relationship with our daughter sent us to the only One Who could give us hope. In the days to come we would rely on the Lord more than we ever had in our lives.

&

Survival Tip

Living with a prodigal will not be an easy life; the road may be long and the destination uncertain. Therefore, don't waste your emotional energy by hoping against all odds that your child will change and suddenly make good choices. Instead put your hope in the Lord. (Psalm 51:17)

&

Suggested Bible Study Characters

David

Hannah

The Woman from Shunem

&

Chapter Nine

𝒮𝒪

Growing Up

Grow up? Now that was music to my ears! Perhaps now Kirsten saw the need for some honesty and integrity in her own life and finally realized she needed some character development before setting out on her own. Maybe she would change her selfish ways and have a tender heart towards God and her parents. If she allowed the Holy Spirit to work in her life, then all we had gone through would be a distant memory. My hopes were flying high once again.

It didn't take long, however, for us to figure out that "growing up" meant something radically different to our daughter. In her mind, she envisioned herself already an adult, and naturally that should include the right to make all her own decisions with no restraints from us. She was exceedingly confident in her own ability to cope with anything life might throw her way. To her, the key to happiness was "freedom."

This was a perplexing time for us. Sadly, one of our worst fears had been confirmed—if Kirsten felt backed into a corner, she might again run away from home. The thought terrified us. We had seen news accounts of what happened to other young people on the run, and we wanted to save our girl from such a fate.

She returned to our home 36 hours after she left, but we were changed parents. Now we found ourselves suspecting her words and doubting her actions. We prayed like we've never prayed before. We asked God to show us what we needed to know and for Him to reveal Kirsten's true nature. We were not able to read her mind and uncover her motives, but God could and did!

Eventually we concluded that our firstborn had become a "double agent." She was not at all the person she tried to portray. She used money specifically set aside for college on frivolous purchases. She lied about her whereabouts and contacted friends in the middle of the night. She obtained a modem and accessed our neighbor's internet without our permission. However, that wasn't all.

She received an inappropriate e-mail while online at my sister's home in California. She bribed and threatened her brother to cover for various activities she knew to be beyond the bounds of our family standards. The more we discovered, the more we became convinced that Kirsten was on a "slippery slope" headed for disaster.

Our once-tight family disintegrated into animosity, resentment, and silence. As we spent so much time on Kirsten, we soon noticed collateral damage to our sons. They resented that nearly every conversation at home, at church, at school, and in the neighborhood centered around their sister. They didn't like being pumped for details by their friends. They were tired of having a mom and dad who were continually sad. They felt we were being too nice to Kirsten while she was behaving so badly. They felt betrayed by her manipulation and lies. At one time, they had admired their big sister—but not any more. They wanted to protect us from additional pain; so they demonstrated their loyalty to us by being angry with Kirsten. Needless to say, our family was falling apart.

We had nearly lost all joy in our home. No one wanted to be there. We felt like prisoners. Someone needed to stay with Kirsten at all times to insure she wouldn't sneak off. We were forced to hide phones and guard purses and cash. It felt as if there were a major crisis every single day. We were exhausted, and Kirsten was stressed. Would we have to be on continual surveillance—forever suspecting every word and every deed? The road ahead did not look promising.

Therefore, we began to search for a mentor for Kirsten. We even searched for a safe place for her to live so we could all recover. She needed professional counseling and spiritual support; we needed respite and hope. We discussed involving extended family or church friends, boot camp, or even juvenile hall, but none of these ideas gave us peace.

As Steven approached open heart surgery, we had grave concerns about how Kirsten might respond when left with just one parent to handle the situation. Besides, the doctor was adamant—Steven needed two full months of stress-free recovery. If we were going to intervene, it must be NOW; we simply could not continue on this course. We felt we had tried every approach we could think of, and to date, there had been little progress. Would our next step lead us to an improving situation, or would it only make matters worse?

&

Reflection

Looking back I remember how exasperating these days were as we watched our beloved child spiral out of control. I often wondered if there could ever be a satisfactory resolution to our plight. Blessedly, God was at work behind the scenes; I just couldn't see it at the time.

&

Survival Tip

Keep reading Scripture, especially the stories of God-in-action. You'll be encouraged as you discover how often He works in amazing ways. (Isaiah 55:9) He is a miracle-working God, and nothing is "too hard for the Lord." (Genesis 18:14)

&

Suggested Bible Study Characters

Job

Lazarus, Martha, and Mary

Peter

&

Chapter Ten

❧

The Last Chance

*P*arenting a teenager was far more complicated than those tranquil days when Kirsten was two. Back then, her strong will could be molded by a stern look, a time-out, a quick spanking, or an offer of praise for obedient behavior. Now we found ourselves way beyond the help of positive reinforcement or corporal punishment. Kirsten had compromised her character, and we could not simply sit back and allow her to destroy herself, her future, or her family. What should responsible parents do with a rebellious teenager—especially one who had the audacity to take off in the middle of the night?

Our situation seemed unbearable, and we asked ourselves, "How long can this go on?" When I allowed fear to rule my thoughts, I pictured her running away again, kidnapped by perverts, and found dead alongside the road. On other days, my hopes soared as I joyfully imagined her freely abandoning her old ways for good choices and truth. Back and forth I went, and Satan worked overtime adding to my emotional upheaval.

We finally came to the realization that we were at a crossroads. Basically the decision boiled down to this dilemma… Do we loosen up or tighten up? Do we allow her to experience the consequences of her choices, or do we eliminate choice from her life in order to insure her safety? Kirsten was obviously committed to Christopher, and we did not want her to feel pushed into a corner where, in her perspective, her only option was flight. She had run off once before, and we were worried she might try that again. Well aware of how critical our response would be, we prayerfully and humbly asked God for His wisdom and direction.

Our prayers were answered when God led us to the Training Center—a nearby facility that had a program for troubled teens. It was a beautiful place. There were plush carpets, lovely paintings, spacious rooms, and nice views. There were no bars on the windows or armed guards marching around a barbed-wire enclosure. However, our major concern had nothing to do with a comfy environment. We wanted something much deeper—a spiritual makeover for our daughter.

We were impressed with the staff. They had been well-trained in Biblical counseling and had worked with many types of teens-in-crisis. In our preliminary interviews, we found them to be caring, perceptive, persistent, and unflappable. We believed if Kirsten were surrounded by godly influences and at the same time, if she were removed from poor patterns of behavior and a few peers who encouraged her rebellion, she would be free to make a turnaround.

Our plans were in place to admit her, but we wanted to give Kirsten one last chance to be completely honest with us. This would require a meeting at a restaurant involving the three of us and Christopher. Our hope was to get all the facts, have a frank discussion, and come to an open agreement about the future of their relationship. We had determined if our daughter were truthful about her relationship with Christopher, we would take her home and give her another chance. On the other hand, if she were not, we would admit her to the Training Center after the meeting. Because we did not want to give her an opportunity to "prepare her story," Kirsten was not informed of the meeting until we were in the car.

The moment the four of us met, Kirsten was worried, and later we understood why. Debacle might be a good word to describe that evening! Christopher shared how he and Kirsten had met, and it was the same version Kirsten had told us—verbatim. We had many questions for him—about his past, his job, his plans with Kirsten, and about what had happened in those missing 36 hours when she ran away. As the two of them glanced back and forth nervously, they became increasingly uncomfortable. We soon realized there was an entire dimension to their relationship that had been deliberately hidden from us. Steven and I were more troubled than ever.

Kirsten was starting to lose her carefully-constructed composure. Her face flushed, and her countenance hardened as she felt cornered. She became unusually quiet—almost sullen, and we knew she was beginning to panic. This conversation was NOT going well, and as Steven and I looked at each other, we knew what we had to do. With heavy hearts, we left the meeting and headed to the Training Center with Kirsten in the back seat.

We knew she would NEVER agree to go voluntarily; to her way of thinking, being sent there would seem like a fate worse than amputation! It was a difficult choice, but we felt it was our only option. Kirsten's life was at stake, and there was no time to waste.

We believed (perhaps naively) that once she was in a safe environment, we could catch our breath and enjoy a bit of peace that had escaped us in the last few months. We also believed once Kirsten had some time to contemplate the seriousness of her recent actions, she would come to her senses. We prayed that the staff would be able to reach her and that God would use their wisdom to change her heart. Perhaps after a few months she could return home and life would be better.

In the next weeks, we were stunned to realize this turnaround would not be quick or easy. Our hopes for Kirsten were well-intentioned, and we were convinced this was God's best place for her, but those two facts did not assure a victory. We succeeded in protecting her and eliminating any chance of liability for her actions, but what we ultimately desired was a heart change. That, however, would never come, unless Kirsten was ready to make that decision herself.

80

Reflection

Looking back I see clearly how God led us to a place of safety for Kirsten, but it didn't turn out as we expected in spite of great counsel. Slowly but firmly, God was asking us to relinquish OUR solutions for the situation.

ॐ

Survival Tip

There may come a time in your journey with an older teen, when you have to quit fighting, manipulating, and strategizing to produce the outcome YOU want. Trust God to find a way to your prodigal's heart when there doesn't seem to be a way. Keep this in mind—prayer indeed does change things, especially in you.

ॐ

Suggested Bible Study Characters

Jonah

Mary

Moses

ॐ

Chapter Eleven

❧

Saying Goodbye

There was a thick silence in the car as we left Christopher at the restaurant. Kirsten wasn't happy with the way the conversation ended, and neither were we. As we drove towards downtown, Kirsten soon realized we weren't going home. We feared she might have attempted an escape if we had shared our intentions; so we waited until the last moment to tell her she had given us no choice—our only option was admission to the Training Center.

My heart pounded as the truth dawned on Kirsten, and I could hardly glance at her. There was so much I wanted to say, but all I could do was sob uncontrollably. This was one of the hardest decisions Steven and I had ever made as parents; obviously it was hard on our daughter too. I had two concerns:

- Would she understand WHY we had to take such a drastic step?
- Would she EVER appreciate what we were doing for her?

Kirsten would be placed in the Center for approximately one year. Two girls would be at her side 24 hours a day to help her and to prevent her from harming herself. She would have the opportunity to work and to complete her junior year of high school. In other words, she wasn't isolated in some cell or deprived of productive activity. She could make some new friends and receive godly advice from people other than her parents. We were so thankful that she would be close to home—about 40 minutes away—and we looked forward to visiting her often. Only God knew that a little girl born 200 miles away and adopted into our home would need such a place when she was 16 years old.

As long as I live, I'll never forget the look of hurt in her eyes; she felt betrayed by our decision. She had no idea how difficult it was for us to leave her there, but after all the upheaval in our home, we believed God had directed us to this place. I kept repeating to myself, "This is best for Kirsten; it will provide protection for her until she's able to make better choices." We were legally responsible for her behavior as she was still a minor, and we were convinced she was not ready to live on her own—no matter how grown up she felt.

As we sat in a private room before our final goodbye, the director asked, "Kirsten, do you really want to make a change in your life? Do you want to be all that God wants you to be?" She paused for a minute, tears streaming from her eyes, and quietly replied, "Yes, I do." At that moment, my spirit lifted. Perhaps God would perform a miracle here, and we would all be on the road to recovery. Such an easy solution was not to be. Our struggle continued—just in different ways.

There were those who questioned our decision, and sometimes we asked ourselves the same thing—did we really have Kirsten's ultimate interests in mind? However, every time we revisited our choice, God confirmed that indeed we had followed His leading. It WAS the best choice for Kirsten; it just wasn't going to be pain-free for any of us.

ဆ

Reflection

Looking back I remember well how confusing and sorrowful this time was for us. We felt as if we had failed completely as parents. I now know this is not true, but in the despair of those days, I couldn't see beyond our inability to reach our oldest child.

∞

Survival Tip

Concentrate on this reality—your value to God is not based on your income, your vocational status, OR the behavior of your children. Your worth is infinite because Jesus loves you and died for you. If you have accepted Him as your Savior, He is currently preparing a place for you to live with Him forever. (John 14:3)

∞

Suggested Bible Study Characters

Joseph

Paul and Silas

The Widow of Nain

∞

Chapter Twelve

❧

The Kidney Stone

It was a beautiful evening, but as we made the 40 minute drive home from the Training Center, we didn't really notice. Our family was divided, and we were an emotional mess. I was distraught that it was necessary to leave our oldest child in the care of someone else. I was furious that some cheeky kid had more influence over Kirsten than the two people who had nurtured her for 16 years. I was discouraged—feeling we had been lousy and ineffective parents. Steven kept asking, "HOW could this happen? WHY did this happen?" I was worried about how Kirsten would handle her new environment with additional restrictions and the lack of privacy. I was numb. We had spent two tumultuous years trying to reach Kirsten's heart, followed by a disastrous confrontation with her and Christopher. It was a very, very, very long and lonely ride home.

Once home, I was shocked when I looked at myself in the mirror! My face was wet with tears. My eyes were puffy and red. I had been carrying five or six shredded tissues that had stuck to my hand. I hardly had the energy to crawl into bed. My husband tenderly kissed me on the forehead and said, "God loves her more than we do. He will take care of her." He held me as I began to cry again. Before we fell asleep, we prayed that Kirsten would allow the Lord to work anew in her heart.

I was having trouble falling asleep as I kept reliving the events of the day. Not long after finally nodding off, I was awakened by a terrible pain in my lower back. I kept tossing and turning, hoping to find a comfortable position. Surely because of the stress of the day, I thought I had probably wrenched my back. As I continued to move around, the pain seemed to intensify rather than subside. I decided to get out of bed and take a walk, but that brought no relief.

At least Steven was getting some much needed sleep, and I didn't want to awaken him. However, the pain was becoming unbearable, and I knew something was terribly wrong. I paced up and down the hall for as long as I could, but I finally had to do something. Steven had been in a deep slumber; so it took a few moments to convince him that I needed to go to the hospital.

As he walked me through the doors of the emergency area, I became violently sick. The nurses whisked me away and gave me a pain shot. Eventually the tests confirmed that I was passing a kidney stone.

As I lay on the cold table, I thought my entire world was caving in. I had said goodbye to my daughter, my husband was having open-heart surgery in a couple of days, and now I was writhing in pain. I cried out to the Lord with question after question.

- When will this all be over?
- Will Steven survive his surgery?
- Will Kirsten be okay?
- Why does everyone else have problem-free children?
- Will I ever live through the night, let alone this next year?

Steven and I had faced other battles before, but nothing was as all-encompassing as this one. We felt helpless and hopeless, and we were tired of the fight. The only option we had left was to utter a feeble prayer: "God, only You can bring good out of this mess. We give up. There is not one single thing we can do; so it's in Your hands now." The pain medication soon took over, and I fell asleep.

℥

Reflection

Looking back I can still feel the depth of hopelessness on this night. It seemed like NOTHING was going right. Not only was I dealing with a runaway daughter and other family issues, I was tormented by excruciating pain. It all seemed so overwhelming. I now realize God wanted me to give up MY fight and allow Him to take over the battle. (Exodus 14:14)

ॐ

Survival Tip

I don't want to discourage you, but it seems that troubles tend to come in waves. Don't be surprised if health and financial issues follow relational crises. Attempt to take good care of yourself, your spouse, and your other children. Solicit an army of faithful prayer warriors to summon help from Heaven itself. When you can't fight any longer, God will take over on your behalf.

ॐ

Suggested Bible Study Characters

Elijah

Job

Moses

ॐ

Chapter Thirteen

&

The Empty Room

We didn't get home from the emergency room until 5 am. I was groggy from the painkiller, and my dear husband was trying hard to be strong for me. We were both physically taxed to the limit. Usually mornings bring renewed hope, but on this particular morning, we felt the weight of the world on our shoulders. Steven had to take part in a funeral, and I had to go to the urologist for more tests. We were both weary and very sad.

I remember walking by Kirsten's room and suddenly it seemed eerily quiet in the house. I wanted so desperately to talk with her and assure myself that she was all right. I called the Training Center and was only allowed to talk to the director. He told me she seemed to be adjusting well to her new circumstances. For some reason, that report didn't ease my troubled heart. I wanted to be able to talk to her myself and convince her of a few truths—that we loved her deeply, that we wanted her back home, and that we were hurting too.

I missed her with every fiber of my being. Our family seemed incomplete without her. The pain of going by her room was more than I could bear. She had left clothes on her bed from the night before. The room smelled of her perfume, and I just couldn't go near it. The necklace my parents had sent for her 16th birthday was on her dresser. Her towel was still on the bathroom floor and her hair bands were on the sink. I found a phone message she had scrawled on a little piece of paper. I even got choked up looking at a half glass of Sprite she had left in the refrigerator. I saw a pair of her shoes in the entryway. I saw dirty clothes in the laundry room and her jacket hanging in the hall closet. EVERYTHING I saw reminded me of Kirsten. I couldn't think. It was difficult for me to even function. All I could do was replay the entire scenario of the night before over and over in my mind.

In addition, I had few emotional reserves to face Steven's upcoming heart surgery. Listening to the surgeon's little speech about all the scenarios that could happen, didn't soothe my mind either. I was totally exhausted and nearly without hope. The next few weeks would be difficult, and God would have to take over, if we were to survive them.

As I fell asleep on the couch, I was awakened by a phone call. My sister wanted to know how we were doing. She gave me a verse that calmed my heart that day and for many days to come. I decided to claim this passage specifically for Kirsten: "I will give them a heart to know me, that I am the LORD. They will be my people, and I will be their God, for they will return to me with all their heart." Jeremiah 24:7 (Later we realized the reference contained the numbers 24/7, and we believed that indicated how often the Lord would be watching over her.)

A few months later I received a prayer in the mail personalizing that Scripture on Kirsten's behalf. This is what it said:

"Lord of all, may You continue to watch over this girl whom we love with all our might. You have placed her in our family by Your omniscience, and our one desire is for her to be all You intend. May You grace her with a tender heart that delights to please and serve You. May she appreciate the depth of Steven and Tricia's commitment and bond to her as she comes to experience intimacy with You, her heavenly Father. Lord, You see the end from the beginning. We do not know the paths she will choose to take, but may we rest content in Your will until the day she decides that Your way is best and she runs to Your embrace."

Steven and I had no idea how well Kirsten would respond to her year at the Training Center. We had no guarantees promised by her counselors. We had no idea why our once-happy and well-adjusted daughter had sunk so far and so fast. However, now we prayed a verse of Scripture on her behalf, and our hearts clung to a promise from God Himself. By the grace of God, Kirsten WOULD return to Him and to us with her whole heart—sometime, somewhere, somehow. We were now more willing to relinquish our timetable for Kirsten's turn around and to trust God. Now we had to wait.

ಬ

Reflection

Looking back I'm encouraged as I review all the ways God was fighting FOR us. Just when I needed it most, He urged my sister nearly 2,000 miles away to call me. He put a verse in her heart that we continue to lean on today. He gave us a personalized prayer from Scripture that expressed our hearts' cry. God was giving us the courage to walk by faith. (Note: I highly recommend *Praying God's Word* by Beth Moore.)

℘

Survival Tip

Keep a notebook dedicated solely to recording all the ways God is at work in your life. Record Scripture verses, comments from friends, sermon notes, lyrics from Christian music, and anything else that keeps your focus on the power of the Lord rather than on the magnitude of your problems.

℘

Suggested Bible Study Characters

David

Paul and Silas

The Disciples

℘

Chapter Fourteen

❦

A Broken Heart

Waiting isn't easy for me. I like to plan ahead, be prepared, and tie up all loose ends as soon as possible. However, parenting a wayward teen was proving to be quite a challenge and obviously a process that would take much longer than we ever imagined.

At the same time, Steven's heart was rapidly deteriorating. I asked myself, "Why did this all have to happen at once?" The date was set for his open heart surgery—September 11, 2002—exactly one year after the terrorists attacked the World Trade Centers and the Pentagon. Although we knew Steven's surgery was in God's hands, the anniversary of 9-11 made that day very sobering.

My emotional energy was depleted from all the trauma with Kirsten, in addition to my own health crisis with a kidney stone. Now my husband, the man to whom I looked for strength, was going to have major surgery. The doctors told us he would need two months of rest at home for a full recuperation. I soon learned if his broken heart were to be successfully repaired, I needed to be strong for him.

We checked into the hospital early in the morning. Several nurses scurried around, drawing blood and hooking him up to various monitors. Steven was very calm that day, and the medication made him oblivious to nearly everything. Just before the orderly wheeled him away to the operating room, we prayed for God's guidance and peace. I kissed him and told him I loved him. As we headed to surgery, I held his hand until I was barred from going further.

The waiting room was packed. Family and friends gathered to wait for news of the five patients who were to have similar procedures. Many church friends came to encourage me and to help keep my mind occupied while we waited. About three hours later, I was elated to hear that Steven was the first patient in recovery; the surgeon informed me personally that everything had "gone according to plan."

I was not allowed to see Steven until he had been taken to the Cardiac Intensive Care Unit. I waited and waited; one by one every other family was reunited with their loved one, but not me. Finally, I inquired at the desk, and the nurse summoned me to a consultation room. The surgeon then reentered the room with a very serious face. He told me that Steven was losing a lot of blood and that the surgical team was unable to find the source of the bleeding. He was receiving a series of blood transfusions and if they could not determine the cause of the problem shortly, he would have to return to surgery.

I desperately wanted to see my husband; so the doctor arranged for me to have a very brief visit. When I walked into the room, I was not prepared for all the additional tubes and machines attached to him. Steven's face was so pale and swollen that I hardly recognized him. To make matters worse, he was unable to communicate with me. After only a couple of minutes, I was asked to leave.

Now Steven wasn't the only one with a broken heart; I had one too. I spent a lot of time on the phone contacting friends and family to inform them of this sudden turn of events. Several more people came to be with me and prayed for us all. I called Kirsten at the Training Center to let her know that her dad's surgery had been successful but that he was bleeding internally. Perhaps realizing that her dad's life hung in the balance she would see the importance of getting her life in order…but such a quick and lovely ending was not to be.

Once again, a passage of Scripture soothed my soul, and I read it again and again over the course of the next few days: "I run in the path of your commands, for you have SET MY HEART FREE."

Psalm 119:32. That word picture gave me strength and hope. While we might not experience instantaneous healing in Steven's heart or Kirsten's life, we KNEW we could trust the Lord. Again, God was calling us to wait on Him.

ೞ

Reflection

Looking back I can still feel the utter helplessness of this day. I was learning that broken hearts of every type are very painful; only JESUS has the power to repair them, and He often operates on us in unconventional ways. God forced me into a place where I could do absolutely nothing but pray and wait.

ॐ

Survival Tip

When you find yourself in an impossible situation, quit scrambling for answers and solutions. Instead, rest and rely on the Lord. After all, "NOTHING is impossible with God!" (Luke 1:37)

ॐ

Suggested Bible Study Characters

Elisha

Joseph

Mary

ॐ

Chapter Fifteen

∂Ͻ

Two Views

It took about ten hours before Steven's bleeding subsided. He remained in the hospital for a week, and then I took care of him around the clock for the first two weeks at home. Needless to say, I was completely worn out. At least I didn't have to worry about where Kirsten was or how she might upset her dad. With her safely in the Training Center, we were able to enjoy some moments of peace. Peace, however, was not exactly what Kirsten was feeling.

We thought we were giving her the safety of boundaries... she thought it was prison walls. We thought of the benefit of counseling...she thought of brainwashing. We thought of the addition of new friends...she thought she had lost all friends. We thought of the opportunity to do different activities to occupy her time...she thought it was torture, having lost all freedoms guaranteed by the Constitution of the United States of America. We saw a fresh start...she saw the end of all life! It's an understatement to declare that she didn't exactly thrive in the Training Center. We had hoped so desperately for a new Kirsten to emerge, but we were to be disappointed anew.

Instead of solving her problems, her reaction to life there only intensified them. We now know this was a period of great struggle within Kirsten's heart and mind. There were many times where she was a broken person who honestly wanted to change. On the other hand, giving up her relationship with Christopher was NOT an option for her. All too often, Kirsten resorted to a new tactic—if she were going to get out of this place, she would HAVE to conform by becoming a "model" of submission, growth, and hard work. Sadly, instead of breaking her patterns of dishonesty, her time at the Training Center only ingrained them.

As we visited her, we sensed things were not right. We had prayed many times for God to reveal Kirsten's heart to us, and He did. We didn't have to go searching for truth; it eventually came to us.

We noticed a tendency for her emotions to fluctuate greatly during our visits. She cried, she begged for another chance, she pouted, she became frantic; later we realized she was trying everything imaginable to persuade us to get her out of there. After a series of tests, a doctor diagnosed her with fibromyalgia. We wondered whether she was really ill or if she was simply trying to manipulate us again.

She was absolutely desperate to get in touch with Christopher. Her father and I had our own desperation too, but it came in the form of questions:

- Does she miss us?
- Does she resent us for putting her there?
- What is REALLY going on in that mind of hers?
- Who is the real Kirsten anyhow?

I was a mess as I wrestled with doubts about my precious child. I had hoped for peace while Kirsten was being nurtured and cared for by godly people, but my heart was crushed to discover that once again, Kirsten was on a mission to deliberately deceive us and the people at the Training Center.

She knew very well the parameters of her stay there. Under no circumstances was she to contact her friends or acquaintances. Our goal was to provide a structured place for her where she could reevaluate her past choices without outside influence. With new skills acquired, she would be able to choose different patterns of behavior and to seek out the types of people who would have a positive effect on her life. Because of her history with Christopher, all communication with him was expressly forbidden.

A few months after her admission, she was caught red-handed. She had managed to trick a friend into "smuggling" a letter out to

Christopher; and when he replied, his letter to her was intercepted by staff who gave it to us. As we read it, our spirits were saddened as we realized our hopes for Kirsten to have a changed heart were dashed once again. She had been quite convincing with her words about "life change," but obviously she was only mouthing what we wanted to hear. The words in the letter fully illustrated that her true intention was quite different; Christopher and Kirsten were hoping to pull off an "escape" and make their future together. It had become abundantly clear—Kirsten was NOT becoming a woman of integrity. She was simply marking time while she continued on with her original agenda.

Again, we were devastated. It seemed no matter how tight Kirsten's boundaries were, she was both smart and resourceful enough to escape them. The issue was ultimately not about a boyfriend; the issue was about honesty and truth. Here she was in a tightly-controlled environment, and she was still calling the shots and seeking ways to circumvent our desires for her life.

The best word picture I can think of to describe Kirsten at this time was a loosely-blown up balloon. When the pressure was applied from one side, she just pushed out the other. How would we ever convince her that she was walking dangerously and that a double-life of duplicity would lead her further away from God's best? We knew the Lord wanted her to have a pure heart and a transparent life, but she was heading in the opposite direction. What were we to do? Would we EVER be able to save Kirsten from herself?

&

Reflection

Looking back I am convinced we made the correct placement decision for Kirsten. She may have resented it and it may not have turned out as well as we hoped, but Steven and I both believe God directed us to the best situation for her protection.

ଅ

Survival Tip

You may second-guess yourself a lot in your dealings with your child. However, don't allow your prodigal to put a guilt trip on you. It's very possible his motives are misplaced. Furthermore, you must be aware that Satan wants to add to your misery by messing with your mind and emotions. If you have overreacted or know you have done wrong, by all means acknowledge it and ask forgiveness. On the other hand, if you have sincerely sought godly advice and prayed over your decisions, then don't look back.

ଅ

Suggested Bible Study Characters

Jehoshaphat

Job

The Woman from Shunem

ଅ

Chapter Sixteen

&

Hope and Help

I don't want anyone to think that every detail of every day was bad while Kirsten was at the Training Center; in fact we have some good memories of those days too. I made every effort to write her notes of encouragement, bring her favorite shampoos or lotions, and slip in some Carmello candy bars for fun. We visited her whenever we were allowed to and took her off-site for holidays and a few excursions.

For Kirsten's 17th birthday, we had a huge celebration at the Center. We sat at the head table in the dining room, and in front of approximately 400 people, we honored her. Steven spoke some precious words about Kirsten's tenacity. He broke down as he envisioned her serving God with that very same tenacity in the future. Family members and friends sent greetings and presents, and we sealed the evening with her favorite dessert—cheesecake.

There were benefits for all of us during her time at the Training Center. The boys were thrilled that the daily drama at home had ceased. Steven and I made a conscious decision to devote ourselves more fully to their needs. Therefore, we made special plans for Spring Break and decided to get out of town and enjoy some adventures tailored to delight our sons. We spent several days in Chicago enjoying Navy Pier, going to a Bulls basketball game, taking a "gangster tour," and gnoshing on Chicago-style pizza. All of us needed desperately to reconnect and to share some light-hearted moments.

Another benefit was that Kirsten was safe; she couldn't run away in the middle of the night and find herself in a life-threatening situation. She was supported and counseled by people who deeply cared about her well-being. In turn, we received counseling as well and benefited greatly from it. When we all met together, it was helpful to have a neutral person guide our dialogue. We hoped Kirsten would grow spiritually and come out of this time more mature, unencumbered by expectations and peer pressure.

Without a doubt, the best part of Kirsten's 14 months away from us was the guidance she received. The curriculum was intense and filled with Scriptural truth and practical application. It was designed to broaden her horizon about her own uniqueness and potential. It offered her a new appreciation for her home life and for our role as her parents. Many of the concepts were not new, but we prayed that they would become more relevant to her. Of course, for Kirsten to fully benefit from her stay she would have to heed the advice she was given; sadly, she ignored much of it.

Some teenagers who run away are sent to juvenile hall. We were grateful that we had another option—a Christian facility less than an hour away from our home. We were equally delighted that her leaders loved her and were pointing her to Jesus. Yes, we experienced many days of great hope and optimism. However, as time went on, we began to wonder…Would Kirsten REALLY benefit from this opportunity, or would she have other lessons yet to learn?

ॐ

Reflection

Looking back I'm glad Steven and I made every effort to maintain a level of communication with Kirsten. I admit there were times when we were so hurt or blindsided by her choices we were tempted to respond poorly. God's Holy Spirit, however, kept prodding us to "overcome evil with good." Romans 12:21

୫

Survival Tip

Whatever you do, keep talking to your child. You might have to bandage your heart after an intense conversation, but at least you have a channel available to influence your prodigal for the Lord. Jesus spent much of His ministry time on earth talking with all sorts of people deemed unsavory because "He came to seek and save what was LOST." (Luke 19:10) The opportunity to share with your child is priceless and could possibly make a difference for eternity; so don't cut off communication, no matter how tempting it seems.

୫

Suggested Bible Study Characters

Rahab

The Woman at the Well

The Woman Taken in Adultery

୫

Chapter Seventeen

❧

Foiled Again

The last few years had sent Steven and me on a tidal wave of emotions—from hope to despair, to hope, to despair again. Now we began to feel our hearts harden towards Kirsten. It seemed to us that every single time we began to trust her words, her actions revealed the opposite. We tried to cling to the promise of Jeremiah 24:7, but our faith was sagging.

I flew to California for my dad's 79th birthday in January. It was fun to meet some uncles and aunts I hadn't seen in years. Because of Dad's declining health, it was a precious reunion. In addition, I was hoping to find some relief from the pressure-packed situation with Kirsten. It was a brief respite from the sadness of life back home.

Kirsten had always looked forward to visiting California in the past, and now I was going without her. She would miss out on all the happy celebrations and the laughter; worst of all, she might never have the opportunity to see her beloved grandpa again. Her face was downcast as I said goodbye.

Now Kirsten was a smart cookie, and although she was capable of navigating any computer system and reciting scientific facts or Bible trivia upon command, she struggled with writing formal papers for school assignments. Hoping for advice and proofreading help and because she was anxious to communicate with us, she faxed a draft of her essay to my sister, an English teacher.

You should have seen the look on my sister's face as she began reading the rough draft. In just a moment she declared, "This is

NOT Kirsten's writing; she has copied this verbatim. In fact, I think I know the source." She returned shortly with a book from her personal library and soon found the original article. I asked myself, "What are the odds of that happening without the insight of an omnipotent God?" We were nearly 2,000 miles away, and of all the Christian books printed in America, my sister "just so happened" to have a copy, "just so happened" to remember the article, and "just so happened" to be able to find it.

When she confronted Kirsten by fax, Kirsten denied any wrongdoing. When that didn't succeed, she concocted an elaborate scenario about sending the wrong computer file. When that didn't fly either, she became hysterical declaring she never could do anything right, no one ever believed her, and she was nearly worthless as a human being. In the ensuing e-mail, Kirsten stated, "I'm faultless before God; so I hope I can stand faultless before you too. I hope you can believe me. I'm sorry I offended you, but it wasn't intentional." It was amazing and so sad that a girl of such promise could stoop so low and go to such lengths to cover up her sin. Would she NEVER understand the value of integrity?

Poor Steven was left to pick up the pieces back home without fully understanding what had taken place in California. My heart was ripped to shreds. After spending so much time in a godly environment, immersed in Scripture and truth, Kirsten could not be honest about something as relatively neutral as homework. How would she ever deal honestly with important life decisions and character issues?

We wondered how deeply Satan, the "father of lies," had ensnared her. We wondered what types of people were affecting her judgment. We wondered what flaws within her personality prevented her from taking responsibility for her actions. We wondered if we were doomed to a life of sorrow and suspicion because of her actions. We wondered how many other betrayals she had contrived without our knowledge. We wondered if we would ever get to anything remotely close to a "normal relationship." Aha—I thought—normal relationship? Maybe that idea would hold the key to everything.

❧

Reflection

Looking back I realize how desperately I wanted my "old life" back. I wanted a happy home with problems as serious as which hairstyles might be acceptable. I had to face reality—life would NEVER be the same again. Miracles are always possible because of God's power, but there would be no return to the "good old days."

৪০

Survival Tip

Expect a new normal. Don't spend all your energy wistfully recalling the past. Face it, you are in a serious spiritual battle. Fortify yourself with Scripture, and discipline yourself to focus on a godly viewpoint. It might even prove beneficial to repeat the following verse several times throughout your day: "This is the day the Lord has made; let us rejoice and be glad in it." Psalm 118:24

৪০

Suggested Bible Study Characters

Elisha

Paul and Silas

The Woman from Shunem

৪০

Chapter Eighteen

&

Off to Florida

*H*mm…normal? Well, maybe after a year in the Training Center, what Kirsten needed and what we needed too, was a good dose of regular, ordinary family life. The past year had NOT been easy on anyone. While we had used the time to recover emotionally and return to a bit of tranquility within our home, we still faced "help" calls from Kirsten, strained visits, and questions by some of our friends. However, we sorely missed our daughter and wanted her back home with us again.

The year had been hard on Kirsten as well. She had been confined to a controlled location without access to media of any type; she had been separated from all her friends—positive and negative alike; and worst of all, to her way of thinking, she had been "kidnapped" away from Christopher.

We wondered with increasing concern, how much longer she would need to stay at the Center and how permanent any "progress" might be. Honestly, we just wanted this traumatic time in our lives to be over! So as we approached our annual family vacation to Florida, we decided to ask permission to take Kirsten with us. We knew she would jump at the chance to "get out of Dodge." When asked, Kirsten's head counselor thought she was ready for a taste of "normal" family life. Perhaps, we thought, when we all were together again, Kirsten would realize how much she had missed her family.

Wonderful is the way I would describe those two weeks. We walked on the beach, had hours and hours of conversation, and really believed much progress had been made in Kirsten's life. She acted perfectly. She was respectful, polite, helpful, and a complete joy to be around. My heart was ecstatic; we were a well-bonded family again at last. She seemed so responsible and mature that my heart began to trust again.

Then the unthinkable happened. We returned from Florida and had one last weekend together at home. We had planned to surprise Kirsten with the news that her release from the Training Center was fast-approaching. We could hardly wait to see her reaction to such an unexpected pronouncement! Kirsten, however, had planned a surprise of her own. She got up in the middle of the night, phoned Christopher, and met him at our back door. Their plan was to spend a few hours together, and then Kirsten would sneak back into her room with no one in the family the wiser.

My mother used to tell me as a young girl that "your sins will find you out." So without any effort on our part, Kirsten's sins truly found her out. Irony of ironies—when she entered a motel that night, she was recognized by the desk clerk. He was shocked to see our daughter walk into the lobby at two in the morning with a young man and then slink out a few hours later. That certainly put him in an unpleasant position. After seeking some advice, he decided to meet with Steven and report what he had observed.

Can you imagine our dismay receiving such a phone call? Instead of happy news and the reunion of our family, we were forced to confront Kirsten again and afterwards return her to the Training Center.

I cannot adequately describe the feeling in the pit of my stomach; I wanted to vomit as I listened to Kirsten vehemently deny wrongdoing of any sort. The clerk then described Christopher precisely and gave a detailed description of the outfit Kirsten was wearing. At last, when backed into a corner, Kirsten admitted being there—with the disclaimer that "Nothing happened!"

My spirit was broken, and all hope I had in recovery evaporated in that instant. I didn't want to even muster a guess about what the future held for my strong-willed and rebellious daughter. How would our family face this new crisis? My hope of returning to "normal" flew out the window, and I once again sank in despair.

❧

Reflection

Looking back I'm thankful this blatant sin was uncovered quickly. We were traumatized, but at least we knew exactly what we were facing. The truth confirmed that the drastic choice we had made to isolate Kirsten at the Training Center had been necessary.

৪০

Survival Tip

Prepare your heart for a tough road ahead. Persistent rebellion, deceit, and self-will in a teenager will more than likely result in grave consequences; hopefully your child's heart will be softened in the process. Do not despair however long it takes because God is working even when you can't see it.

৪০

Suggested Bible Study Characters

Jacob

Samson

The Prodigal Son

৪০

Chapter Nineteen

❦

Trusting Kirsten

After a sleepless night, we wearily trudged off to the Training Center with Kirsten in tow. As we reviewed the episode at the motel with her counselor, Kirsten was very contrite and remorseful. She cried and stated emphatically, "Now I know Christopher is NOT the man for me. I need more time here so I can be better prepared to deal with the freedoms and responsibilities of life at home."

So Kirsten returned to the safety of the surroundings at the Training Center. During this last stint, she was accommodating to the suggestions of her counselors, and her words indicated a change of heart. She said Christopher was a closed chapter in her life, and we sincerely hoped she was on the road to maturity and growth. At the end of just one month, her counselors decided to release her to us. We were overjoyed and praised God for hearing our prayers.

Because of her strong academic bent, we began to talk to her about going away to college. We felt if she had a goal to work towards, she would have enough incentive to continue making good choices. We helped her prepare for her college entrance tests and were elated when she passed her ACT's with high marks. We encouraged her to apply to a Christian college a few hours away, and we all were thrilled when she was accepted into the nursing program. It was a fun time of bonding as we took a few shopping trips to purchase clothes for her new life at college.

It was at this time I received some hard news from California. My dad, who had been diagnosed with Alzheimer's a few years earlier, suffered a serious setback and had to be placed in a rehabilitation facility. With a heavy heart, I flew across the country to be with my mom. Upon my return, Steven met me at the airport and said Kirsten had a confession to make. My heart dropped.

While I was away, our neighbor mentioned to Steven that he thought someone from our family was a lead-footed driver. That morning while he was jogging, a car sped by, ran a stop sign, and nearly hit him. There was no mistaking the vehicle. There weren't any other older blue Hondas with Purple Heart insignias on the license plate in the neighborhood. Since both boys had been working, I was in California, and Steven was at church, there was only one conclusion—Kirsten, unlicensed, had taken our car without permission and had gone on a little joy ride that possibly could have cost a man his life.

There was, however, a glimmer of hope—Kirsten immediately had taken responsibility for her actions. Although there were plenty of horrible events that MIGHT have happened, God had protected her. In addition, her forthrightness about this incident encouraged us that maybe now she had at least learned to be honest.

It was wonderful having the family together again, and we looked forward to celebrating Thanksgiving, Christmas, and her 18th birthday. We were thinking that perhaps we had made it through the worst part and were, at long last, beginning to trust Kirsten again.

80

Reflection

Looking back I sometimes ask myself, "Was I too quick to trust my daughter after she betrayed us again and again?" I've come to this conclusion—NO! A mother's love should be "patient" and "kind." It should "always trust," "hope," and "persevere." A mother's love should "never fail." (1 Corinthians 13:4-8)

৪১

Survival Tip

Follow the example of Jesus Who prayed from the cross, "Father, forgive them, for they do not know what they are doing." Luke 23:34

৪১

Suggested Bible Study Characters

Peter

The Woman at the Well

৪১

Chapter Twenty

&

Eighteen at Last!

The future looked bright, and Kirsten was looking ahead. We decided to visit the college she planned to attend. She enjoyed the five days immensely, and Steven and I were delighted to see hope once again shining in her eyes. She participated in several activities and spent each night in the dorm. The students were wonderful and even managed to find a ticket and an evening gown for her so she could attend a formal event with them on campus. Kirsten seemed to be on Cloud Nine!

She said her time there confirmed in her heart that this was the place God wanted her in the fall. She was adamant about the choice. She mentioned she loved being around such good, clean, wholesome fun, and she could hardly wait to begin her studies there. Before college, however, Kirsten had her final semester of high school to complete.

She was excited about her approaching 18th birthday in January and the fact that she would finally be "legally classified" as an adult. We wanted to honor her on this important milestone and made plans for a wonderful celebration. We had all been through some very trying days; therefore, we wanted to let her know how pleased we were of her progress. As we envisioned her going off to college in a few short months, we wanted this occasion to serve as encouragement and affirmation.

Shortly after Christmas and before her actual birth date, we invited approximately 30 of her friends to celebrate. We brought photo albums of Kirsten from her baby days to the present, and the young people had fun reminiscing about the "good old days." Laughter filled the room, and she talked freely about joining many of them at the same university in the fall. Despite the fact that her relationship with some of these kids had been put on hold during her time at the Training Center, they were there in force to communicate their support. Watching her that evening, it was obvious this party was a success.

We were breathing much easier these days, and we didn't feel as though we had to monitor her every single move. Steven and I had the opportunity to attend a music conference three weeks before her actual birthday. It looked like the perfect time for the two of us to get away and relax. It did cross our minds, however, that Kirsten would need some accountability and supervision in our absence; so we arranged for her to stay with a responsible couple. I will never forget her last words to me. "You don't have to worry about me doing something stupid. I'm not going to run away, Mom. You can trust me." We set off to enjoy the serenity of the mountains, little knowing that new trauma lay ahead for our family.

After six days of singing praises to God, renewing friendships, and basking in the beauty of God's creation, we headed for home. When we got about halfway there, Steven's cell phone rang. As I listened to his side of the conversation, my faith, hope, and joy plummeted; one more time, Kirsten had betrayed our trust by running off with Christopher. Our friends found this note left behind by Kirsten, "Please don't worry. I'm okay. There is a note on my bed at home that will tell my folks where I am." We were totally stunned and devastated, especially after a search of her room produced no such note. Despite her assurance, we had no idea where she was. If it hadn't been for our faith in God, I don't know how we would have coped.

When we had admitted Kirsten to the Training Center a year before, we thought that was the very LAST resort; now what were we to do, and where were we to go? Apparently nothing would prevent our daughter from carrying out her personal agenda. She had desperately wanted to be on her own and free from any parental restriction, and now sadly, she had gotten her way.

As we mulled over this latest development, we realized there was not much we could do. The prayer of our hearts went something like this: "Lord, what's the next step for us as parents? Do we just let her go, or do we fight to get her back? You gave her to us and we love her, Lord…BUT PLEASE TELL US CLEARLY…WHERE DO WE GO FROM HERE?"

❧

Reflection

Looking back I'm not sorry we gave Kirsten an opportunity to experience a taste of college life. I'm not sorry we planned a lovely birthday celebration. I'm not sorry we gave her opportunities to make good choices. I am sorry, however, that she was so determined to obtain her "freedom."

∞

Survival Tip

There comes a point in the life of many prodigals where parents lose all physical control over their children. This is the time the adult may learn what it REALLY means to walk by faith and not by sight. Deliberately make the decision to relinquish your children to the Lord, and tell yourself again and again, "God loves them more than I do!"

∞

Suggested Bible Study Characters

Hannah

Jonah

Mary

Shadrach, Meshach, and Abednego

∞

Chapter Twenty-One

❧

Fifteen Days of Silence

It is hard for me to explain how awful the next few days were. My heart hurt, my head hurt, my stomach hurt; and I could barely function. Steven was distraught and kept asking, "WHY would Kirsten do such a thing?" We thought she had made such progress, and now our hopes evaporated.

As we walked by her empty room, our emotions were on a veritable teeter-totter. Our grief was nearly unbearable. We felt betrayed and duped. We thought we were the most foolish parents in the world to trust a daughter who had run away before. HOW could she do such a thing??? We felt guilty for going away. To complete our misery, we were scared as we considered the precarious situation in which Kirsten might possibly find herself. After that we simply cried and cried and cried and cried and cried.

The worst part, however, came as I recalled some of her last words to us. "You can trust me; I won't run away." I remembered all the wonderful conversations we had about her changing her life, her plans for college, and her hopes for the future. I remembered how she talked so convincingly about "closing the door on past choices and friends." All of her words seemed to haunt me, and I replayed them again and again in my head. Now her actions undercut everything I thought I knew about my daughter. I beat myself up trying to figure out the truth about our relationship with Kirsten.

We came home on a Saturday night, and the following evening we decided to share our burden with our church family. I don't know if I can adequately express how difficult this was for Steven and me.

We had tried to be strong and had made every attempt to handle this situation ourselves. However, our world was crashing around us, and we definitely needed many people praying and standing alongside us if we were going to survive the next few days. It was very humbling to let everyone see how broken our "perfect little family" had become. We were overwhelmed by the response. For nearly an hour, our friends personally waited to hug us, encourage us, cry with us, and pray for us. What a blessing to be surrounded by such a powerful show of support. At the same time, however, we were emotionally drained and sick at heart.

Over the next several days, word continued to leak out about Kirsten, and we were surprised to learn new details about her last few weeks. Eventually we came to the conclusion that Kirsten had been living a double life all along and had carefully and cleverly led us astray in order to be with Christopher.

After a brief lull, our brains went into high gear as we tried to reassess our situation. Before we made any new decisions, we had to gather all the facts. We suddenly realized we didn't even know Christopher's last name. Where did he live? Could we find any of Kirsten's friends to help us? Where in the world did our daughter go? Why did she pick such a time? Why couldn't she talk to us before she took off on such a desperate course? There were times we thought we were crazy as our thoughts careened out of control.

Eventually I discovered that Kirsten had a cell phone, and I obtained her number. I left message after message for her, but there was no response…nothing! We were hurt that she refused to contact us. After several days of agony, we learned she had been in contact with a neighbor of ours, and so we asked her to intercede for us. This lady was very tenderhearted and had used Kirsten as a babysitter many times. She was willing to be an intermediary and to provide a safe haven if Kirsten needed it.

Although it was awkward, we used our neighbor to deliver the following letter for us. We hoped Kirsten would read it again and again. If our spoken words did not get through to her, hopefully God would penetrate her heart with our written love.

January 13, 2004

Dear Kirsten,

From the moment we first laid eyes on you to this very minute, we have loved you with all our hearts. Through the years you have brought us great joy, and we are so grateful to God that out of all the homes in the whole world, He lovingly placed you in ours!

These last two years have been difficult for you and for us too. We know we are not perfect parents and we have made mistakes, but we believe we reared you the best we knew how. We cheered you on, we took you all over America, we gave you a good education, and we instilled in you a love for music. We played with you, we spanked you, we hugged you, and we even gave you two brothers. We prayed over you and with you, and we laughed together many times. We were honest with you from the start about your adoption and have always been very grateful to your birth mother for her sacrificial love. We sent you to camp and gave you your own purple bedroom in your first house. We surprised you on your 16th birthday with unique love gifts and even gave you your 18th party a month early to accommodate your long invitation list. However, our MOST important desire was this—we wanted you to know who Jesus was and more than anything, we wanted you to be a member of His family. For all of these blessings we are indeed thankful.

Now here we sit in our home without you, and we are very sad. We are sad because you felt you couldn't tell us the truth about your life, and we are sad you felt you had to leave home. We do not want the distance between us to continue; so now what are we to do?

All we can think of is...KIRSTEN, WE LOVE YOU STILL!

Although we haven't chosen this path for you, we have decided to give you the freedom you have longed for in order to make your own decisions and to put on your shoulders the responsibility to accept the consequences. You have chosen your path, and we wish you God's best. He loves you more than we ever could because He is the One Who made you to be the Kirsten we adore. He is with you everywhere you go, and He will be the Answer to all your deepest needs. Since you are no longer in our care, we lovingly place you in His hands.

All our love,
Mom and Dad

P.S. We would love to meet you for lunch. Just let us know when and where. We want to hear your heart.

From the time we received that horrible phone call until the time I saw her face to face, it was 15 very long days. Steven and I held our breath to see just what she would say and how she might justify her actions. How should we talk with a girl who deceived and hurt us so badly? What should we say? What should we omit? How should we treat a young man who carried our precious daughter out of our life?

We had a lot of questions and pain, and we were afraid our words would tumble out so intensely we might lose our daughter forever. I know what my flesh wanted to do and say, but in spite of our hurt, we still wanted to act the way Jesus would. We just weren't sure how.

Reflection

Looking back I smile at the letter of love we penned to Kirsten; that idea was truly Spirit-directed. We later learned she read it often, thereby sending our devotion to her even when we weren't nearby. However, we didn't possess a letter of love from her, and we were often unsure of our place in her life. The words of Scripture were our ONLY measure of consolation.

৪০

Survival Tip

Spend time studying the people of the Bible. You'll discover that:
- None of them lived perfect lives.
- Many of them faced uncertain circumstances.
- Several of them made poor choices and big mistakes.
- God often surprised them with love and grace (and sometimes even a spectacular miracle).

Put your hope in the promises of Scripture and the power of God.

৪০

Suggested Bible Study Characters

Jehoshaphat

The Man Born Blind

৪০

Chapter Twenty-Two

❧

Face to Face

There is nothing worse than not knowing where your child is. So when we found that Kirsten was safe, we felt some peace. HOWEVER, our fears mounted as we began to anticipate that first meeting with her. We sincerely wanted to do what was right, but at the same time we were upset and wounded deeply. Our concern was this—would this meeting lead to healing or to further estrangement?

The day finally arrived when we were able to meet Kirsten face to face, but it was not to be on our terms. We were informed that we must now consider Kirsten and Christopher as a team and that they had moved in together. She would visit us in our home on one condition—that Christopher had to be accepted as part of her life. On one hand, we HAD to welcome him if we wanted anything to do with our daughter, but on the other hand, we had half a mind to "clean his clock." We agreed to abide by Kirsten's requests, but we needed lots of prayer to get us through this next phase.

In the interest of peace, Steven and I had decided to let her have some clothes and other personal items. When Kirsten and Christopher walked through the door, I completely lost my carefully-crafted, cool demeanor. I sobbed uncontrollably. I opened my arms and held her very tightly. I didn't want to let her go knowing that in a few minutes she would be leaving us and that NOTHING would ever be the same again. I also made every effort to welcome Christopher even though my heart was saying something else.

I had to come to terms with the facts—Kirsten would turn 18

in three days, and at that time we would have no legal recourse. It was imperative that we begin to restore our relationship with her. We knew if we scorned her or scolded her, it might cut off further communication. It felt very awkward as we slowly walked up the stairs. Conversation was forced. We weren't certain what to ask, and there sure were some topics we didn't want to know anything about. Steven struggled even more than I did, and my heart broke as I watched him attempt to cope with the very real loss of "his little girl."

Kirsten was more interested in moving items out of her room than talking through the issues that had resulted in this rift in our family. Obviously this was NOT the time to say most of the thoughts rambling around in my head. Steven and I had decided it was better to say little or nothing at all rather than to say something we would regret later or something fake. Therefore, words were painfully few that evening.

We watched as she went through every drawer in her room. Her heart was revealed by what she took and what she left behind. She took clothes, makeup, shoes, and hair products. She left behind her Scripture Memory trophies, Bible study books, and the American Girl doll we had sacrificially given to her years before. It appeared she deliberately tried to extinguish all traces of her spiritual heritage and to leave behind any tender memories of life with us. It seemed my heart would break. Apparently Kirsten was on the fast path to a new life and image.

We were further appalled when she threw away all evidence of her sophomore, junior, and senior years of home-education. She was one term paper away from earning her high school diploma, not to mention we had forked over hundreds and hundreds of dollars for her education. Foolishly, she believed she would never need proof of her last three years of academic work.

Kirsten was doggedly determined to move on with her life. One look at her face was enough to show us we could not reason with her this night. The only option left for us to do was to wait until she was finished in her room, say goodbye forever to all our dreams for her, and sob ourselves to sleep after she left.

We thought our pain was severe before, but this was new territory for us. Would we EVER be able to forgive her? Would we EVER be able to accept Christopher in our lives? Would our hearts EVER heal from this ordeal? Would we EVER be able to trust Kirsten again?

Our energies would now be consumed by the healing process. Without Kirsten in our home, we didn't have to worry about where she was, but of course we did! We had to find some way to connect with her so we could have an impact on her new life. Now we had a mission. Regrettably, that would prove to be much easier said than done.

⁐

Reflection

Looking back I have no regrets about the comments I didn't say. God was teaching me many lessons on this journey, but one of the biggest was this—YOU DON'T HAVE TO SAY EVERYTHING THAT COMES INTO YOUR MIND! The night Kirsten moved out of our home was the lowest point yet, but the Lord helped us maintain a relationship with her BECAUSE we said very little that night.

ço

Survival Tip

If your child has a hard heart, you cannot penetrate it by piling on the words, no matter how brilliant they may be. Once your prodigal breaks away from your home, keep your opinions to yourself. When I'd get ready to deliver another lecture on a certain topic, Steven would whisper, "SYB" (Save Your Breath). I needed a reminder that it's only the work of the Holy Spirit that can break a stubborn soul.

ço

Suggested Bible Study Characters

Peter
The Woman at the Well
The Woman Taken in Adultery
(Note how few words Jesus used to
convict people who were living in sin.)

ço

Chapter Twenty-Three

&

The Start of a New Relationship

After Kirsten moved her belongings out, Steven and I were faced with a dilemma—what did God want us to do now? Should we try tough love and put more distance in our relationship, or should we attempt to build a bridge between us and Christopher and Kirsten? To be candid, it would have been easy to dump all the blame for Kirsten's missteps on Christopher, but that would NOT have been objective or pleasing to God. Besides, that course would have obliterated any attempt to reconnect with our daughter.

We wrestled with our thoughts. Some people thought an ungrateful and cold-hearted daughter should be left alone to reap the consequences of her actions. However, God wouldn't let us do that. We were convinced He wanted us to fight for her soul and spirit with every ounce of our being. Therefore, we deliberately chose to reach out to Kirsten, even though that was the riskiest approach; after all, we had been rejected by her more than once. The main issue here was this—we did not want her left alone to flounder without the benefit of our guidance. She needed us now more than ever, even if she didn't know it, even if she didn't want us.

I called Kirsten and offered to take her to lunch at a nice restaurant she loved. I arrived first and watched as she whipped into the parking lot and came to a sudden stop. My brain immediately formed this question in my head—"Did she now have her driver's license, or was she driving illegally?" The answer to that question would be left for another day.

When the newly-liberated Kirsten stepped out, I was astonished! In just a few months she had morphed from what looked like a sweet, wholesome teenager to someone I hardly recognized. Apparently she wanted to break every dress standard we had tried to impart. Even the look on her face portrayed hardness. Was this the NEW Kirsten? Was this the REAL Kirsten? Eighteen years of parenthood had not prepared me for this kind of transformation, and I'm sure my face and eyeballs registered my shock!

Our conversation was stilted and uncomfortable. I wanted to establish some line of communication, but I hardly knew what to say. All Kirsten could do was rattle on and on about Christopher, his family, her freedom, her choices, and her friends. If I interjected any news about our extended family or those who had invested in her life since childhood, she disregarded it. She declared she had never been more happy. To tell the truth, I had never been more sad.

I had a difficult time masking my emotions and attempting to put up a good front. I begged her to consider coming home again, but she would hear none of it. I burst into tears, and she used that as an opportunity to leave abruptly. I was left sitting alone in my booth wondering if it was worth it to try to maintain any kind of connection with her at all.

I didn't know if my heart could take any more bruises, but at least I had made the effort, no matter how feeble. Kirsten would NEVER be able to say that I wrote her off or quit on her! That day was tough, but God gave me the strength to take that first little step. I initiated the meeting knowing it would be unpleasant and hurtful, but I can unequivocally say it was the right choice to make. How could I ever hope to be a spiritual influence on her if I slammed the door shut?

ℬ

Reflection

Looking back I clearly see how important it was to meet with Kirsten. Although the occasion was painful for me and didn't seem to have any value at the time, it was a start. To this day, we meet regularly and talk on the phone often. Our relationship is much deeper now, and so are our conversations. None of this would have been possible if I'd refused to have any contact with her because I disapproved of her choices.

છ૭

Survival Tip

Keep the long view in mind. Ask yourself, "Is the way I'm treating my child today going to push him farther away from me, or is it going to leave the door open for his eventual return?" Listening to your prodigal's heart may be distressing or unpleasant for you, but it may be better than never hearing from him again! Also, you may be the only level-headed person in your child's life and the only testimony of Jesus.

છ૭

Suggested Bible Study Characters

Jonah

Lazarus, Martha, and Mary

છ૭

Chapter Twenty-Four

🕭

In Touch with the Past

Adoption is a source of great joy and celebration, especially to moms who have struggled with the pain of infertility. I must say, however, it also complicates certain aspects of parenting, particularly when children reach their teen years. Many young people try to figure out "who they are," and this issue can be especially difficult for adoptees.

We told Kirsten from the time she could talk that she was adopted. She especially enjoyed looking through the small photo album that told our story of waiting, filling out reams of paperwork, interviewing, and driving to pick up our new baby. We celebrated her birthday every January 31, and we celebrated her adoption day just as merrily every September 29. For some reason, Kirsten seemed to have lots of questions about the details, and we didn't always have every answer. Nevertheless, we gave her as much information as possible.

The adoption agency originally told us that Kirsten's birth mom had requested that her baby be placed in the home of a pastor. In addition, this young mom communicated with us through the adoption agency several times. She always asked about Kirsten's progress, and I tried to keep her informed. Obviously she had a depth of love and concern for her child that seemed unusually mature.

When Kirsten reached junior high, her adoption questions grew more intense and specific. We told her we would be happy to help her search for her birth mom when she was finished with college and on her own; that way she could handle some of the details of her conception and birth with more objectivity. By then, she would hopefully be settled in her own adult life.

Besides, we had heard all the horror stories. Some birth parents never wanted to know their children, and some had lived horrific lives of pain and failure. Often adopted children had no specific information about their heritage and, therefore, fantasized that out there somewhere was the most beautiful, successful, wealthy mom the world had ever known. It was with great reservation we approached the idea of reunion, and we wanted to be right there with our daughter when that happened. Kirsten had always assured me she would include us should she begin her search.

Now that Kirsten had moved out, she wanted all the papers we had collected during the process of her adoption, and we reluctantly gave them to her. Because of our precarious relationship, was this the best timing? Was my daughter mature enough to handle the possible complications? Did this mean she was about to replace me with a new mother-figure? I was crushed. Resourcefully, she called the agency for additional details and was soon in contact with her birth mom, Kari. They corresponded through the agency for approximately three months. Then Kirsten registered her personal information online with hopes of finally meeting Kari in person. Respectfully, Kari called us to ask our permission before making direct contact with Kirsten.

At the time, I was reeling from the death of my father. I flew to California to help Mom adjust to life without Dad after 59 years of marriage. Wouldn't you know it—that's just the time I learned that Kari was asking to meet Kirsten. This new development caught me offguard, and I was unprepared to deal with it.

Questions flooded my mind. What kind of woman was she? How would Kirsten portray us as her parents? Would Kari be sympathetic to what we had been going through with Kirsten? What kind of advice would she offer? Would Kirsten reject me and our 18 years together? What role would I now play in Kirsten's life? Would Kirsten wait until she was older as we had agreed, or would she rush off to meet Kari in person before I returned home?

Suddenly I felt very insecure, and the emotional trauma of the last few years hung over me like a storm cloud. I was nearly 2,000 miles away and had absolutely no control over Kirsten or what would happen next. I stewed and fretted, but my sister reminded me that all of my worrying was pure speculation. After all, Kari did give us the courtesy of calling for our approval, and just perhaps she would turn out to be a godsend not only in our lives, but in Kirsten's as well.

That day I read these words in my Bible study: "Thoughts about the future are, at best, only guesses. Furthermore, the future is in God's hands—His loving capable, merciful, powerful hands. He can enable us to deal with what is real, with what is not, and He will be with us whatever the future holds." (*Loving God with All Your Mind* by Elizabeth George, p.33)

Faith is trusting God without knowing the way ahead. That's exactly what He wanted me to do. It wasn't the way I had planned it, but through the circumstances, God forced me to relinquish Kirsten and to let her go on without me.

ஓ

Reflection

Looking back on this chapter, I can almost hear Jesus saying in my ear, "Tricia, Tricia, Tricia. You are worried about many things, but Kirsten's birth mom should NOT be one of them." I used up a lot of energy as I contemplated so many negative thoughts that would result from a premature reunion, that I barely considered the possibility that Kari might be an answer to my prayers. At the time I had no idea what a blessing she would prove to be—not only to me, but to Kirsten as well.

ℰℴ

Survival Tip

There may be days where the future looks bleak, especially after you've battled long and hard for your teen without apparent success. When you are exhausted, you probably won't have the strength to consider other outcomes. However, remember…God is amazingly creative and powerful. Don't limit His ability to bring blessing out of any state of affairs. (Romans 8:28)

ℰℴ

Suggested Bible Study Characters

Jehoshaphat

Joseph

Mary Magdalene

Shadrach, Meshach, and Abednego

ℰℴ

Chapter Twenty-Five

&

A Meeting of the Moms

Before I could return home, Kirsten and Christopher made a beeline to meet Kari. I was devastated because it felt like my own daughter was shutting me out of one of the most important moments in her life. Instead of taking me, the one who diapered her, rocked her, cheered her, and taught her for 18 years, she took her boyfriend who had only known her two years. My emotions were traumatized anew. In my worst moments I imagined a glorious reunion for them coupled with a total rejection of me.

Kirsten was elated, and when I returned home, she glowingly described Kari's entire family. On the one hand, I was relieved, but on the other hand, I brooded over my place in this now-complicated relationship. I spoke on the phone with Kari a few times, and her calls were surprisingly assuring to my heart. We made plans to meet soon.

In some ways, I felt like I knew Kari before I saw her face. Years ago when we first considered adoption, we were well-aware that in order for us to have a baby, someone else had to give up a baby. At the time, my sister was teaching school. When she shared the joy of Kirsten's arrival, one student was perceptive enough to ask prayer for the birth mom. We continued to pray for this brave and unselfish girl over the years, especially on Kirsten's birthday. We had always wondered if we would EVER meet her, and now we were getting ready for her visit.

Kirsten received several pictures of Kari as a child; everyone was amazed to see the similarities. I made copies of them and began putting them in a special album for Kari. Her pictures were on one side of the page, and pictures of Kirsten at the same age were opposite them. There was no mistaking the gene pool!

We invited Kari and her husband Peter to our home so we could meet them in person. All my fears vanished as we talked. It was hard to fill in 18 years of memories in a couple of hours, but we wanted to give them a flavor of our life with Kirsten, including all the difficulties of the last few years. Kari had a serenity and wisdom that were well beyond her years; she was like a sponge soaking up every detail of Kirsten's life. How foolish I had been to lose sleep over the impact she might make in all our lives.

Suddenly we were aware that God had put our families together for a common goal. We were thrilled to hear of the strong Christian heritage of Kari's family that went back several generations. Kirsten's birth grandparents had prayed every single day for that little child who had been removed from their lives.

Kari could have undermined our authority, manipulated Kirsten, and made life difficult for us, but that was NOT her goal. She constantly assured me by saying, "Tricia, YOU are Kirsten's mom, and we are praying about the role God wants us to play in her life so that we can also help her." They were grateful for how we reared Kirsten and couldn't stop thanking us. Their words and actions soothed my soul then…and still do.

Now we had more partners in our ministry to Kirsten. Instead of a fiasco, God joined Kari's heart to mine and would bless all our lives more than we could ever imagine. Just think, we were two women separated by 27 years and 120 miles. Our lives had taken distinctly different paths, yet our hearts beat in sync for the daughter God had given us both. Only the LORD could have orchestrated such a life story!

ॐ

Reflection

Looking back I stand amazed at the unexpected way God worked in our lives. I believed Kirsten's attempts to find Kari would prove to be a heartbreak, if not a complete disaster. How wrong I was.

ᛒ

Survival Tip

Never underestimate the power of God to create a blessing out of any situation. Do you remember when the children of Israel, fleeing Egypt, were caught between the armies of Pharaoh and the Red Sea? (Exodus 14) How many of them could have imagined such an amazing escape—that God would part the waters opening a pathway through the sea? When you feel like giving up, read Psalm 77:11-20.

ᛒ

Suggested Bible Study Characters

David

The Disciples

The Man Born Blind

ᛒ

Chapter Twenty-Six

&

Another Dip on the Road of Life

Kari did not have the history with Kirsten that we had, and she was very optimistic about influencing Kirsten in the right direction. With our blessing, they spent a lot of time together. One day, Kirsten surprised us with the news that she and Christopher had decided to live apart. What's more they intended to move close to Kari.

Originally we hoped the change would be for the best, and at the same time give Kari the opportunity to make up for lost time. I was saddened that Kirsten seemed to disregard my perspective on her life, but at least she was listening to wisdom from Kari. I was thankful for that.

Christopher and Kirsten had shared bank accounts and living arrangements. Kari and Peter, however, proposed a new plan—Kirsten could live with them, and Christopher could purchase and live in a small trailer nearby. Kari and Peter found good jobs for both of them, and Kirsten enjoyed getting to know her new family which included three more brothers.

Kirsten relished being with Kari. Christopher had the opportunity to live on his own and to begin a credit history. With high hopes, Kari and Peter set out to guide this young couple. All went well for about seven months, but sadly, some of the same issues we had encountered soon bubbled to the surface. They discovered that adding a new-found daughter and boyfriend into their family proved to be much more complex than they had anticipated. As time went on, the relationship became increasingly intense, and after a confrontation,

Kirsten and Christopher packed up their belongings. Christopher moved back in with his dad, and Kirsten moved into the trailer. How ironic that Kari and Peter experienced the identical trauma we had and were left reeling. It wasn't long before Kirsten moved back in with Christopher's family where they could at last experience the latitude they desired.

This was an unsettling time for Kari's family and for ours. We prayed long and hard, often wondering what the future held for our daughter. We brainstormed a variety of ways to get Kirsten's attention, but she was a very strong-minded young lady and would have to learn by experience. At least now, we had four adults working together to resolve the situation instead of just Steven and me. However, we were left with the question—where would this new road take Kirsten in the days to come?

ಬಿ

Reflection

Looking back I see that unless the Lord intervenes in a mighty way, some situations take an extraordinarily LONG time to repair. I was growing so weary of the fight and of the unknown in dealing with our child that I just wanted it all to be over and done with, sooner rather than later. God, however, was not only teaching my daughter many lessons, He was teaching me as well! There are many situations you can control, but for those issues beyond your power, you must patiently wait.

∞

Survival Tip

Be prepared to treat the experience with your prodigal more like a cross-country race rather than a 50-yard dash. Some children are very stubborn and—like certain nuts—must endure a lot of pressure before they crack. However…don't be disheartened. The Lord can develop many wonderful character qualities IN YOU as you wait on Him. (Isaiah 40:28-31)

∞

Suggested Bible Study Characters

David

Hannah

Job

Joseph

∞

Chapter Twenty-Seven

&

Destination: Marriage

Once my precious daughter set her mind on a course of action, nothing short of a miracle would stop her! Kirsten's dream was to marry Christopher, and her indomitable spirit was apparent as she continued making plans. At this point, we weren't nearly as convinced as she was that an impending marriage would be in her best interests. We were pleased she had completed her high school education with a GED, but we believed that her academic potential was much greater. She was young and had a lot to learn about life. Our greatest concern, however, was that she had forsaken her spiritual roots, and we believed she would never be as happy as God intended her to be until she surrendered her heart and will to HIM.

Before they moved back by us, Kirsten and Christopher had approached us about getting married. They were sweet as they asked for our forgiveness about their past indiscretions and stated their desire to make a new start with our blessing. We recommended premarital counseling, urged them to wait several months, and encouraged them to continue to live apart. Regrettably, Kirsten and Christopher reverted back to their old ways and were once again living together. We asked ourselves how honest was their apology? Their words and actions did not seem to match. Kirsten forged ahead with her wedding plans.

We felt hemmed in on all sides and didn't quite know what to do. She was fully emancipated and could legally do whatever she wanted. Not wanting to ostracize her or push her away from us, we just stepped back and allowed her to choose her own way. We much preferred our daughter married than living with her fiancé. If we were going to continue to be a part of her life, we realized we couldn't fight her any longer. One action we could take, however, was to pray, and so we prayed like crazy—again. I remember praying with all the faith I could muster, that God might intervene and prevent Kirsten from marrying Christopher at this time.

As many prospective brides do, Kirsten spent more time making wedding plans than thinking about her commitment for life. Other thoughts troubled my heart as well. Would Christopher be able to support her? What would happen if Kirsten soon became pregnant? Did they have medical insurance? If they both had minimum wage jobs, would Kirsten EVER be free to fulfill her educational dreams? Once again, however, the quandary that most disturbed us was spiritual—would this home be established on a firm godly foundation that would buoy them along over rough times and give them the peace and purpose they both desperately needed?

Weddings can be filled with anxiety under the best of circumstances. Merging two different families from a couple of generations with different heritages and goals can be stressful with all of it being compounded by nerves, finances, and details about the ceremony, honeymoon, and new residence. In our case we had the added complication of more family lines than normal, Kirsten's recent choices, and our role in a wedding we could not fully support. We were struggling.

We prayed and prayed and prayed. God heard our prayers but did NOT answer according to OUR will. I was convinced that somehow God would prevent this wedding from taking place. Why didn't He? I felt like I was going over Niagara Falls without a barrel, spinning out of control. How would I ever be able to make it through the ceremony? It was supposed to be the happiest day in my daughter's life, and I could not embrace her joy.

I shopped with Kirsten for her wedding dress and bridal registry. Even those occasions, however, caused me great pain because many of her choices were diametrically opposed to the way we had reared her. Steven was crushed and was in turmoil about the service; how could a dad give away his daughter to someone she'd already given herself to? Her brothers had been hurt as well and were angry about the damage their sister had caused our whole family. Sadly, no family members participated in the ceremony.

Our church friends were asking many questions, and there were times we didn't want to say a word. We didn't want to vilify our daughter or damage our hopes for having a good relationship with her and Christopher in the next few months. Kirsten and Christopher were about to make their relationship permanent, and that would open a new chapter for us all.

🙰

Reflection

Looking back I recall how difficult these weeks were for me, mainly because Kirsten wasn't heeding Biblical principles for her life. However, I had to face the fact that I was no longer part of her "chain of command." Nevertheless, I am very thankful our family was there and worked in many ways to show her unconditional love.

℘

Survival Tip

Pray for God to give you clear direction for difficult moments—for example, when to fight and when to let go; when to offer help and when to refrain; when to speak up and when to clam up. Also remember you are NOT required to answer every question that is raised about your child's choices. Be honest, but feel free to say something like, "I'd rather not say right now, but please pray for all our family. We need direction, discernment, and courage."

℘

Suggested Bible Study Characters

Elijah

Jehoshaphat

Moses

The Prodigal Son

℘

Chapter Twenty-Eight

ॐ

Here Comes the Bride

The wedding weekend was finally upon us. Our home was a swirl of activity as we hosted family members, made lists, and tried to be accommodating to Kirsten.

The rehearsal dinner was somewhat awkward because there were several branches of Kirsten's birth and adoptive families. Kirsten and Christopher served a lovely lasagna dinner. A very sweet moment came when Christopher presented Kirsten with a unique gift that was a reminder of the musical training of her childhood. He had purchased a flute as a special surprise for her and he was beaming as she played for us all. Both bride and groom went out of their way to welcome everyone and express their thanks.

During the rehearsal, I watched from the back of the church as Kirsten orchestrated all the details of the ceremony. When she was small, I had often dreamed of this day, and little of it matched my expectations. This was not our church, our pastor, our music, or our family in the wedding party. Besides, it all happened much sooner than I had envisioned and on different terms. Once again, God was asking me to relinquish my hopes and dreams. Would I fake a smile and babble on and on about her wedding day, or would I just sit and sob uncontrollably? I had worried that I might not make it through the day, but God began to soften my heart and prepare me for a brand new stage in my life as a mom. I realized there needed to be growth in MY life about trusting God, letting go, and giving unconditional love no matter what my personal opinion was.

The evening served as an opportunity for Kirsten's birth mom, birth dad, and birth grandparents to express their feelings. They went out of their way to specifically say THANK YOU to us—not for the wedding, but for the 19 years we had invested in Kirsten. Their worst fears about what might have happened to that little baby placed in an unknown home vanished as they had the privilege to witness a personable, capable, and resourceful young woman get ready for married life.

The next day, Kirsten was a beautiful bride, and it was apparent to all that Christopher loved her very much. Despite the delicate situation, all the pictures of the various family groupings went off without a hitch. With a relatively small amount of money, Kirsten and Christopher had a lovely wedding and reception. Kirsten had produced a wonderful video of her childhood and of Christopher's as well; watching it brought back many good memories for everyone there. The couple looked very happy as they set off on their honeymoon. As I returned home that evening, I admitted to myself that Kirsten wasn't the only one who had much to learn—Steven and I did too.

Many aspects of Kirsten's life were now completely beyond our control, and we would have to wait on God to do His work. It would take time and prayer to bring healing, but it was time for us to come up with a deliberate plan to reach out to the newlyweds. Life was not about our wishes, goals, and dreams. Kirsten and Christopher had made a permanent commitment before God and man, and we needed to support them.

Steven and I now had a choice about how we were going to treat them. No longer were they rebellious teenagers; they were young adults trying to make a new life together. They needed our support. God was calling us to make some serious changes in our attitude and perspective. How could we get close enough to influence their lives? How would God take this shaky start and turn it into something lasting?

℃

Reflection

Looking back at my heart that day, I remember struggling to keep my composure; it didn't seem like the "happily-ever-after" I had once imagined. However...God was calling us to change our perspective and our tactics. This road we were traveling would continue to have its share of surprises, and only one truth was absolutely certain—God was walking alongside us every step of the way, and we would survive this journey.

ॐ

Survival Tip

Be willing to try new approaches appropriate to your situation. However, there are no guarantees about what strategies will succeed with your prodigal. Sadly, some children don't return for a very long time...or ever. In every case, whether your situation is easily solved or not, your job is to pray for wisdom to do what is right and to trust the Lord with the rest.

ॐ

Suggested Bible Study Characters

Cain

Jonah

Samson

Shadrach, Meshach, and Abednego

ॐ

Chapter Twenty-Nine

❧

Turning Point

Kirsten was now a married woman, and Christopher was a permanent part of our family. We had a responsibility before God to be the people GOD wanted us to be. Now we were going to have to relinquish our hurt feelings and make every effort to bridge the gap.

There are a lot of books and seminars about rearing babies and parenting teenagers, but where is help for a brand new mother-in-law? How did I want Christopher to remember me and my influence on his life? Did I want to act like Jesus, or did I want to hold on to my own expectations? This would prove to be a time of great soul-searching for Steven and me as we walked into this new chapter of life.

We made a prayerful decision to change our hearts first. There are certain attitudes we would just have to release. Instead of dwelling on the past, we would look ahead. It was obvious that Christopher indeed loved Kirsten and had many endearing personal qualities. He was trying to be a part of our family and went out of his way to please us. How could a mom not love that? If we were ever going to be spiritual mentors in any way to this precious couple, we had to begin now.

At the same time, we were realistic about the difficulties they would face as a couple. They were young, had very little money, and no insurance. They didn't have their own living quarters, and both had forfeited further education for the moment. Although they were paying their bills, they pretty much lived from week to week. On the other hand, we were more settled in our lives and were well aware of what difficulties could happen in just a moment. It was so easy for us to worry and fret, but that route was certainly not productive.

All of us would have to learn to walk by faith. Our trip would not prove to be an easy stroll around the park; instead it would be more like a grueling marathon. I had to come to grips with the idea that God was at work in all of our lives and that He had many adjustments for us to make. My "perfect" plans for Kirsten had been blown to bits, but I was feeling hopeful again. Then our daughter dropped another bombshell!

⁝

Reflection

Looking back I see this time in our life from the perspective of a person standing in the open door of an airplane waiting to skydive and experience the total terror of free fall. That is the best image I can conjure up to describe TRUST—jumping out into the great unknown. (May I suggest here that you have an extended discussion on the comparison between having extreme faith and skydiving. Note: Those who have never tried either, use the word "terror" while those who have, use the word "exhilarating.") I will say that when we did take our "leap of faith," we met God in a way we'd never known Him before. He became more real, more faithful, more precious. We would leave this experience changed forever, and that would be an unexpected blessing.

⁝

Survival Tip

God is the Creator; therefore, His approaches are infinite in dealing with every circumstance of life. In particular, study the Gospel accounts of the life of Jesus, and watch all the ways He interacted with people, even those who were up to their camels' knees in sin. Ask the Lord to give you His eyes, His heart, His methods as you enter your own uncharted territory.

&

Suggested Bible Study Characters

Jehoshaphat

Jonah

The Woman at the Well

&

Chapter Thirty

&

Oh Baby... Oh Boy!

*B*eing a parent of married children was obviously a new experience for Steven and me. Kirsten and Christopher needed our love and support, not our suggestions (no matter how glorious they might have seemed to us). We were both teachers—by profession—and it was so easy for us to talk a lot. We also had been diligent about pouring wisdom into our children, but now we had to learn the art of giving advice ONLY when asked. Regrettably, we weren't asked as often as we would have liked!

Although we had concerns about their finances, jobs, living situation, and maturity, our primary prayer for Kirsten and Christopher centered on their spiritual welfare. WHEN would God get a hold of their hearts? HOW would God get a hold of their hearts? Obviously, we would have to trust His timetable and His ways.

One day Kirsten called and said she and Christopher had to speak with us. She had something to say and refused to give us a hint as to the content; she wanted to meet us in person. The tone of her voice was ominous, and my mind began racing to places that were scary. (Please note that I just said we were learning to trust God, and this was about to be another new lesson for us.)

We invited them over for a nice dinner, but I couldn't quit wondering what could be so important. Steven and I tried to act like nothing concerned us, but we wanted to just cut to the chase. Kirsten and Christopher didn't seem troubled...but WE were. Finally Kirsten blurted out, "Mom, we're going to have a baby!" They were delirious with joy.

Do I need to mention that our perspective was slightly different? Immediately our practical, seasoned, realistic minds went to no money, no house, and no insurance. Christopher was having trouble finding steady work, and Kirsten had bounced around from job to job. They had been down a rough road in their own personal relationship, and now had been married just two short months. We asked ourselves, "Is it asking for more trouble to bring a child into this mix?" Could we be as delirious with joy as Christopher and Kirsten were? Once again, we had to relinquish something—our well-intentioned ideas about their family plans.

We made a serious attempt to put a good face on our true feelings. Although we were sobered about this new responsibility, we believed God wanted us to have His perspective. We were reminded that children are a heritage from the Lord. (Psalm 127:3) We weren't really ready for this news and were overwhelmed by the complications it could possibly bring. Nevertheless, Steven and I vowed to do everything in our power to love this little child and to fill his mind with truth.

The next nine months were a blur of activity. Kirsten thrived on all the excitement. She read books, registered for baby items, took Lamaze classes, and eagerly anticipated her new role as a mom. Christopher was equally elated. Kirsten was blessed to have several lovely showers, and so all my worries about how this young couple could afford outfitting a new baby quickly dissipated. (Note to self: Why worry? God takes care of us.)

I found myself looking forward to the birth more and more as each day passed. At last, Kirsten and I had many PLEASANT topics to discuss. One very special day, Christopher and Kirsten called and invited me to a sonogram that would reveal the gender of our first grandchild. Thoughtfully, Kirsten included her birth mom Kari, as well as Kari's mother; so all together, we met baby Camden for the first time. My heart melted at the sight of that tiny baby sucking his thumb in utero. What a miracle given to us by God! I also was able to see Christopher in a new role—dad. He wept and wept, overwhelmed at the sight of his son. In a mysterious way, God was beginning to weave our hearts together.

Life was beginning to seem more positive. Kirsten and Christopher both found steady, full-time jobs. They also realized the importance of establishing their own identity in their very own apartment. They moved into a new place about four months before the baby was born.

Basically Kirsten's pregnancy went smoothly, but after minor complications, the doctor decided to induce labor on April 25, two weeks early. This date was not an accidental choice. God used it to emphasize Kirsten's spiritual heritage. This was Kari and Peter's wedding anniversary. In addition, my dad, who loved Kirsten dearly, went home to be with the Lord after a relatively short bout with Alzheimer's disease on that date exactly two years before. They had a unique bond, and he always believed she would come "back to her senses" even in the darkest days. He faithfully prayed for her through the years. Now what a happy occasion this date would ever be for all of Kirsten's extended family.

Kari, Peter, Steven, and I met Kirsten and Christopher at the hospital. I was so excited, but I had no idea what to expect. Remember, I was an adoptive mom; so all of this birth experience was as new to me as it would be to Kirsten. I was in for the ride of my life.

We were all in the labor room experiencing every contraction and fetal heartbeat. However, at one point, the numbers dropped to such a low level that the doctor decided to take action. The nurses scurried around, and the level of tension rose substantially. The doctor said, "It's time to go...NOW!" Immediately Kirsten had to make an instantaneous decision. Only two people were allowed in the delivery, and without hesitation, Kirsten asked me to join her and Christopher. My insecurities about where I stood in Kirsten's heart evaporated. That moment will stay with me forever.

Words cannot describe the emotions I felt. I was proud of my daughter's strength. I was heartened by Christopher's joy and pride.

I was thrilled at my grandson's cry, and I was grateful to God for the miracle of life. God had indeed blessed our family and had renewed our hope. Steven and I committed ourselves to invest in Camden's life. We fully intended to be faithful and prayerful grandparents delighting in the "gift" God had just given.

෮

Reflection

Looking back I can plainly see that the birth of this baby would soften all our hearts and provide impetus for a closer relationship among us all. And to think my initial reaction to his conception was so skeptical! If life had proceeded according to MY plan, we would not be grandparents as soon; we would also miss an opportunity to serve our children and influence the next generation.

ℬ

Survival Tip

If you choose to remain in a negative frame of mind, you just might push away your children when they need you most. You might also miss out on the opportunity of a lifetime. Delight in the surprises God sends your way; you can't begin to imagine how He can take something you deem unwise or wrong and miraculously turn it into a blessing.

ℬ

Suggested Bible Study Characters

Joseph

Lazarus, Martha, and Mary

Shadrach, Meshach, and Abednego

The Man Born Blind

The Woman from Shunem

ℬ

Chapter Thirty-One

&

A Weekend to Remember

Our little grandson brought joy everywhere he went, and Steven and I loved our new job as grandparents. It is amazing, however, how much we had forgotten about babies. They are so snuggly and so loving; they are so dependent and so hungry; they are so expensive and so worth it! As we had the opportunity to rock him, we prayed that he would be given a deep spiritual heritage and that he would come to know Jesus at an early age.

Kirsten and Christopher obviously adored their son. They doted on him and wanted to follow "all the rules" about child-rearing. Kirsten enjoyed her maternity leave, but soon had to rejoin the work force. Life suddenly became more stressful; after all, now there were three people to think of and care for. The constant demands of a newborn coupled with the huge life-events of the last 12 months were beginning to take their toll. I sensed there was tension building in that little home.

As I began to think about Christmas, I asked myself what would be an appropriate and valuable gift for them this year. Money was tight for all of us, but sometimes a mom has to splurge and start planning very early. God impressed on my heart that Kirsten and Christopher were at a crossroads and desperately needed some time away. As I listened to a Christian radio station, I heard about a marriage conference coming to their area, and we decided to send them. They would have the opportunity to "get away from it all." Of course, our hope was that they'd be able to sit under some godly teaching. Little did we know the impact of that Christmas present.

There is no doubt that God was at work. We obtained the approval of Kirsten and Christopher, secured reservations at a five-star hotel, arranged for babysitting for Camden, and collected gift cards from extended family to make their weekend more affordable. We put this together in August, happily looking ahead to October. None of us were totally aware that this couple would be at a crisis point in their marriage exactly one week before the conference.

Kirsten and Christopher attended all the sessions. They heard in a fresh way about God's design for marriage and the unique role of a husband and a wife. They learned tips for communication and how to put Christ at the center of their home. The weekend ended with them making a commitment to faithfully attend a good church and live in obedience to God's Word. If you would have asked me two years before if such a heart change were possible, I'd have said NO! However, it was crystal clear upon their return that they had definitely changed.

From the beginning, Steven and I had been concerned about Christopher's salvation—had he accepted Christ personally, or was he just going along with Kirsten? We could never quite pin him down on the details. On the way home from the conference, Kirsten point blank asked him. Christopher shared that after talking to Peter one weekend, he had trusted Jesus to be his Savior two years before, and he was clearly able to share his experience. This was the most wonderful news anyone could ever hear!

We saw a more tender spirit between this young couple, and Christopher expressed a desire to be a better husband to Kirsten. She, in turn, realized she had some adjustments to make in her own wifely responsibilities. We sensed they were headed in the right direction. At long last, our little family felt as if we were ALL on the same page. After what we had been through, that in itself was a miracle. It was the beginning of a new relationship with Kirsten, Christopher, and Camden.

The conference was titled "A Weekend to Remember."* Indeed it was.

* The conference title, "A Weekend to Remember," is used by permission from FamilyLife.

∽

Reflection

Looking back I'm grateful the Lord urged us to keep looking for ways to reach our daughter. There were many days that I was so exasperated I wanted to give up, but the example of Jesus kept tugging at my heart. There was not a prodigal that He wouldn't love. I wanted to be like Him.

୧୦

Survival Tip

Surround yourself with people who will hear your heart, encourage you, and brainstorm with you new ways of reaching out to your child. In addition, solicit prayer support so you can discern between enabling the sin and supporting the sinner. Your ultimate goal is to make opportunities available for your prodigal to return to the Lord with a whole heart. (Jeremiah 24:7)

୧୦

Suggested Bible Study Characters

Jacob

Jehoshaphat

Moses

Paul and Silas

Peter

୧୦

Chapter Thirty-Two

☙

A Fresh Start

To be honest, there were moments when I wondered if the changes I was observing in Kirsten and Christopher were real. I had no desire to be suspicious or cynical, but we had been fooled before, and we were well-aware Satan hadn't given up on his goal to wreak havoc in our family again. This walk of faith was as much a lesson for our children as it was for us. Our only hope was to step back and put our trust in the Lord.

We prayed as much for Kirsten and Christopher now as we ever did. This time, however, we began to see many glimmers of hope. They started coming to our church, without any prompting from us. They seemed to enjoy coming over for dinner afterwards and spending more time with the family. It was apparent they desired the best for Camden and actually initiated talks on parenting. Imagine! Their jobs proved to be stable, and they began construction of a new house. It was exciting to see God work over the next few months.

One Sunday we began discussing the possibility of Camden being dedicated to the Lord. Christopher wanted to know what all was included in such a step. We explained that, in reality, it's not the children who are dedicated but the parents; they make a commitment before God and man to rear their children according to the principles of Scripture. It is a serious and public vow which cannot be entered into lightly. We noticed that Kirsten and Christopher seemed to give it very careful thought.

We were absolutely thrilled when Kirsten and Christopher

decided for themselves to take this important step. For a family with as many branches as Camden has, it took some planning to come up with a date where everyone was available. December 17 was a landmark day in the family history. It was also an incredible day in the life of Kirsten's birth mom. For 19 years she and two preceding generations had prayed for Kirsten, and now they were a part of a family committing itself to the spiritual welfare of Kirsten's child. Four generations of believers were united in a common goal. What a godly heritage that little boy has!

That was a precious day. I will never forget the joy and smiles; it was a powerful reminder to me that Kirsten and Christopher had come a long way in the last few months. God was also prompting me to make some changes myself, relinquish my doubts, and allow God to continue the work in all of our lives.

&

Reflection

Looking back this day gave me such hope. Remember, "nothing is too hard for the Lord." (Genesis 18:14) I realize I have repeated this verse, but I needed to read it again and again. Wherever you are today on your journey, be faithful, continue to pray, and keep your eyes on the power of the Lord, not the problems of your child.

&

Survival Tip

God is in the business of salvaging people from the messes they make in their lives. Where people might see junk, He sees potential treasure! Ask God to give you a fresh new perspective of your child and his future.

&

Suggested Bible Study Characters

The Prodigal Son

The Woman from Shunem

&

Chapter Thirty-Three

❧

An Unexpected Gift

*W*hen I began this book, I had no idea where it would end. Would we ever be restored to our daughter, or would we walk farther and farther apart because of tension and distrust? While our story continues to be a work in progress, we have many blessings for which to be thankful.

One day I suggested to Kirsten that we plan a surprise party for Kari who had walked her own complicated path through her teen years. Remember, Kirsten's birthday had always been a day of great celebration for us, but for Kari it brought back sad memories of saying goodbye to a little baby many years before. As Kirsten's 21st birthday approached, she made the decision to forgo any presents for herself, so that all the gifts could honor Kari. After all, Kari is an unselfish and unassuming lady, and Kirsten wanted that day to be all about her birth mom. The more Steven and I thought about it, the more we agreed—with one condition—we did not want such a hallmark birthday to go unnoticed for our daughter. Therefore, we plotted some surprises for Kirsten as well.

Kari is an amazing woman, and we are continually grateful for her gracious gift of Kirsten to us; so Steven and I joined the fun with enthusiasm. Kirsten contacted all the relatives—far and near, biological and adoptive—and we began our very great strategy. She collected money for four unique and special surprises for her birth mom:

- A European massage
- A steak dinner for two at an upscale restaurant

- A carriage ride through our city's historic downtown
- A night's stay at an elegant hotel

Kari thought the party was a surprise for Kirsten; so she was flabbergasted to hear everyone yelling surprise when she walked into the room. Each gift was met with tears and great joy. To cap it off, Steven read (or attempted to read) my letter to Kari expressing my gratitude to the Lord for bringing us all together.

Dear, dear Kari,

Happy birthday. Steven and I are so blessed to be related to you—by heart and soul. God has taken us both on an incredible journey, and only He could have written such a conclusion (even though we're not finished yet).

As an adoptive mom, I faced several insecurities—like what kind of person Kirsten's birth mom really was and if Kirsten ever met her, where would that leave me? Needless to say, those fears were completely groundless.

Your character and calm have been a wonderful example to me. I have learned from your wisdom and steadfast faith in God. Your commitment to Kirsten and your consistent prayers for her through the years have provided a foundation for her to rebuild her life. There is no way I can express my gratitude for the ways you have supported Steven and me in rearing OUR daughter. Instead of replacing me, you have teamed with me. Together we are better parents than we would have been alone!

May God continue to bless your life. Joined at the heart, we are Mothers and Grandmothers Forever!

With Love,
Tricia

By the time I could get my emotions under control, I said, "There's one more surprise." Kirsten responded with, "No, there's not." Little did she know that the last surprise was for her.

Kirsten could not take jewelry when she entered the Training Center; so I had been wearing the five-diamond ring that we had given her five years before. Each time I looked at it, I was reminded to pray for her. This night was Kirsten's birthday celebration too, and we wanted to remind her anew of our love for her. Therefore, Steven and I decided this would be a perfect time to give the ring back to her. I had taken it to a jeweler to be cleaned and polished, and so it was sparkling and beautiful.

What fun it was to wrap it in six boxes, each one a little bigger than the next. As Kirsten was given the large present she had no idea of the contents. She waded through all the boxes and the suspense built. When she opened the last one she crumpled in surprise and joy and happiness. She couldn't compose herself for a while. Finally she said, "I never thought I'd get it back." We hugged and we cried, and then Steven read another letter.

Happy Birthday, Kirsten,

Twenty-one years ago we embarked on a very great adventure called parenthood. Little did we know what would lie ahead, but we were ecstatic and humbled. "Regular" parents have to take what they get, but God intervened in a miraculous way and hand-picked a unique child specifically for us—YOU! (In His goodness, He would repeat the blessing two more times.)

Our extended family was captivated by your mounds of curls and boundless energy. We loved being Mommy and Daddy and poured our lives into you and your brothers. The years rolled by, and our minds are filled with memories of laughter and vacations and school and music and church and God's blessings.

As you know, five years ago on your 16th birthday, we found ourselves in more difficult waters. Despite the situation, we wanted to convey to you how very much we loved you, and so we planned five surprises for you. We don't know who enjoyed the festivities more—all of us "conspirators" or you. Remember Aunt Susie jumping out of a box in the basement and your dad driving very fast along country roads in the canary-yellow Mustang? Remember running up to Erika's door to show-off the car and instead being surprised yourself by all your friends?

We reserved the best present for last. We scrimped and saved to buy you a ring that would always remind you of our commitment to you. It had five diamonds nestled together—we saw that as a symbol of five Bradleys staying close. We carefully considered what we wanted to engrave inside and settled on two characteristics of God—Purity and Honesty—which we wanted to pass on to the next several generations. Sadly, our journey together in the next few years was less than ideal, but we NEVER stopped loving you or praying for you or wanting to restore our relationship with you. When you left our home, sadly, the ring stayed behind.

Well, tonight as we honor your 21st birthday, we would like to return the ring to its rightful owner. As we do so, we want to again remind you of our love for you and our commitment to you, our firstborn child. Our fondest hope is that you become all that God has created you to be. You are embarking on a brand new year anticipating a brand new house. You and Christopher have also recommitted yourselves to Christ and each other, and we see your future as very bright. So again on a special birthday, we present you this ring as an enduring reminder of our hearts. May Purity and Honesty guide your every decision, and may you wear this ring with joy. We pray that your spiritual heritage and your Bradley roots are forever embedded in your life. Never forget… you are well-loved, by God and by us! Blessings to you, our dear daughter.

We love you,
Mom and Dad

As I relive that moment, all I can humbly say is that God has been VERY good to us. He was with us through the uncertain times, and His love sustained us when there seemed to be no hope. That night we rejoiced that there was progress in our relationship with our once-estranged daughter. We firmly believed the Lord had brought us full circle and had answered our prayers for reconciliation. We can't predict what the years ahead will hold for us, but God has brought us a long way, and we owe any praise and glory for that to Jesus Christ.

Recently, we enjoyed a ladies' luncheon at Kirsten's new home. We were joined by Steven's mom, my mom, my sister, Kari, Kari's mom, and Kari's aunt. We had a wonderful time laughing, eating, and taking way too many pictures. As Kari's mom observed the bonding among us, she remarked that this day was "an unexpected gift."

I've treasured that phrase in my heart since then because I think it describes our journey these last few years in a new context. The unexpected gift of barrenness has become the joy of adoption. The unexpected gift of shattered expectations has become the joy of trusting God's ways more than mine. The unexpected gift of loving a prodigal has become the joy of ministry to others in a similar situation. The unexpected gift of trials has become the joy of a deeper walk with the Lord. The unexpected gift of a divided family has turned into the joy of reunion and the opportunity to cement a heart-bond with people who were once strangers to us.

If you are walking down an uncertain road today, I trust God will use my story to encourage you and give you hope. Only God can rebuild and restore broken lives. Psalm 30:11-12 says, "You turned my wailing into dancing; you removed my sackcloth and clothed me with joy, that my heart may sing to you and not be silent. O Lord my God, I will give you thanks forever."

ଚ୦

Reflection

Looking back I'm amazed at God's goodness to our family. Our relationship with Kirsten continues to grow, but we can't predict the future. We do know, however, that no matter what happens, the only way to survive is to relinquish our own aspirations and instead put our hope in the Lord. (Psalm 42:5)

&

Survival Tip

Never, never, never give up! God can bring hope out of despair, peace out of turmoil, joy out of sorrow, and life out of death.

&

Suggested Bible Study Characters

Lazarus, Martha, and Mary

Shadrach, Meshach, and Abednego

&

Chapter Thirty-Four

♥

Kari's Letter: "Thank You God"

*K*ari has always given us her full support—including her approval of this book. Here is a note from her so that you, the reader, can have a glimpse into the heart of this very unique and dear woman.

> *At seventeen years of age, I was in a situation where I felt like I was outside of myself looking in on someone else's life. I couldn't believe what I saw happening...I was pregnant. The reality of it all didn't begin to sink in until I was about four months along. I felt as if I'd disappointed so many of the people I loved the most. What would I do? How could I face everyone? Although this was a very stressful time for my family, my parents were there for me with their godly wisdom and love. They helped me to get good Christian counsel, and I spent a lot of time praying and seeking God's will as I decided what I should do next.*
>
> *It was important to me that what ever I decided to do, be in the best interest of my child, but also be a decision that I could live with. I wanted to do what God wanted me to do. I gave the whole situation to Him because I just couldn't bear the burden of this life-changing decision myself. I came to the conclusion that this baby was going to need a loving, Christian, two-parent home. I didn't know it, but God already had a couple lined up who had been longing for a child to love and care for. God began to guide my heart toward the decision to place my baby for adoption. Choosing adoption was the hardest decision of my life, but I felt*

totally at peace about this choice and still do today. I can say that I have never regretted this decision just because of how much peace I felt in the fact that I had totally sought out God's will in my decision making process.

*"**Thank you God** for being there for me to lean on. You took my burden and carried it for me. Thank you that I could rest in the fact that You are God, You love me, and You are in control. Thank you Mom and Dad for guiding me to godly counsel and supporting me in whatever decision I made."*

After placement, there were some times that were hard for me. Some of the hardest were on Kirsten's birthdays. I would imagine a family somewhere celebrating another year with their daughter, and it felt bittersweet. On that day I would always take out the only picture I had of my baby and say a prayer for her. When I would go out, I would look for little girls with curly blond hair and blue eyes who were about her age, just to get an idea of what she might look like and wonder if just maybe I could be looking at her. It was also hard those first few Mother's Days without her. I was a mother, and yet I wasn't. I did correspond with my baby's adoptive parents a few times confidentially through the children's home, and felt so much comfort in knowing she was doing wonderfully.

*"**Thank you God** for filling me when I felt empty and for making me joyful when I felt sadness. Thank you Steven and Tricia for the encouraging and comforting updates on Kirsten. Thank you for letting her know that I placed her with you because I love her and wanted the best for her."*

At this point in my life I was probably the closest I'd ever been in my relationship with Jesus. I was wholeheartedly seeking Him in my life now and wanted to do what pleased Him. Some time later I was baptized and requested a song to be sung by the congregation when I came out of the water. The words conveyed how Jesus can make one beautiful and can use anything to draw others to Himself. This is exactly what I wanted my life to do.

Today Kirsten, Tricia, my mom, and I all wear bracelets that say "Something Beautiful."

"**Thank you God** for bringing things into my life that cause me to seek You more and become closer in my relationship with You. Thank you God that in Your hands You can make everything beautiful."

Eighteen years later I got a call from the children's home where Kirsten was placed. She had made contact with them, and she was interested in making contact with me. I was excited and nervous all at once. The questions started to accumulate in my mind. Could I finally be getting a chance to learn everything that I'd been wondering about her for so long? What would she BE like? What would she LOOK like? What was going on in her life? On the other hand, what would she think of ME and the fact that I didn't keep her? How would my husband and three boys handle the whole idea of her coming into our lives? What would people who never knew I had an unplanned pregnancy be thinking? Would they be judgmental? What did Steven and Tricia think of our meeting? Would they feel threatened by Kirsten getting in contact with me? Would they prefer that I just stayed out of the picture? Could God really be allowing me to be a part of her life after all?

Our first meeting was by phone. I was nervous and didn't know exactly what to say. When she figured out it was actually me on the other end of the phone line, I could hear the excitement in her voice. We arranged to meet face to face very soon after that. The big day finally came on June 26, 2004. My family went outside to greet her, but I watched from inside the house as she got out of her car to come up to my home. The resemblance was remarkable! She looked so much like me, as well as her birth father. Neither one of us could hold back the tears. After so many years I was finally able to hug my baby again. All the answers to my questions came rushing at me faster than I could absorb them all. After our reunion we went to my parents' home where she

met my parents, brothers, and all their families. It was so exciting
for everyone to get to see the baby girl, all grown up, that we'd
been praying for and wondering about for so long. My thoughts
were changing from thinking of her as someone I may never meet,
to now beginning to develop a relationship with my daughter. I
could see how after being obedient to God, I was now reaping
rewards. I was prepared to have to wait to see Kirsten until I got
to Heaven, but God was giving me such an awesome blessing by
allowing me to meet her here on earth.

    "**Thank you God** for making it possible for me to meet my
daughter. Thank you Peter, for taking Kirsten in with loving
arms as if she were your own. Thank you to my boys for accepting
Kirsten into our family as the sister you never had. Thank you
Kirsten for loving me and for the amazing effort you put into
having a relationship with me. Thank you Steven and Tricia for
letting Kirsten be free to be reunited with me even though you
were not sure what would happen to the relationship you had
with your daughter."

    After the "honeymoon" period of our initial meeting, there
were some struggles that started to arise. When Kirsten and I met
she was dealing with some tough issues in her life. She'd made
some choices that she and I both knew were not godly and that
went against everything she had been taught as a child. These
choices were not only affecting her but were now affecting me and
my family. Peter and I weren't sure how to handle a lot of what
was happening. Our oldest son was 13 at the time, and we hadn't
had to deal with some of the issues that come with an 18-year-
old girl. We wanted to respect her adoptive parents and try not to
take their place. Again, we turned to God for guidance, and He
was there for us. I'm not going to say that it was easy, but I've
learned that I tend to grow more in the struggles brought before
me. I believe God placed Kirsten back into my life in His perfect
timing. Perfect for me and perfect for her. For reasons unknown
to me, my family and I were having an influence in Kirsten's

life that she needed at that time. We were now partnering with Steven and Tricia in lifting her to the Lord and influencing her with an example of seeking after God's heart in making good choices. Up until now, my only influence had been in prayer; now I had the privilege of being able to communicate with her face to face. Although it was somewhat stressful at times, what an honor it was for me to be able to be involved in her life at such a critical time.

"**Thank you God** for loving me and providing what I need when I need it in Your time. Thank you Peter for struggling through all the issues we faced with Kirsten, right along with me, and staying by my side when things got tough. Thank you Steven and Tricia for giving me the opportunity to be an influence in Kirsten's life and for all the godly teachings that you instilled into her at an early age."

Since our reunion, several years ago now, I've been blessed to be able to be with Kirsten through some of her biggest life events—her wedding, purchase of a new home, and the birth of their first child (I'm a Grandma!). There have been very few days that I haven't talked with Kirsten by phone, e-mail, or in person. Our relationship continues to grow closer, and I can't imagine life without her. My husband and I have a good relationship with Steven and Tricia, and we consider ourselves to be partners together in our prayers for Kirsten. Kirsten is a beautiful, smart, outgoing, caring, and loving person. I love her very much and feel so blessed to know her. It has been so good for God to put her back into my life.

"**Thank you God** for Kirsten and the special gift that she is to my family and me. Thank you for all the extended family that loves her and who have prayed for Kirsten since before she was born. Thank you for the relationship I have with Kirsten and her adoptive parents and the unity I feel with them. Thank you for such an awesome unexpected gift."

⅜

Chapter Thirty-Five

&

Kirsten's Letter

*S*ome of you may be curious about how Kirsten actually feels about the publication of her story. Here is her candid perspective.

Have you ever seen a corn maze? It is very intriguing, but once a person is committed to a particular path, he has no idea what the outcome may be. I think that describes my journey over the last few years. Like most good parents, my mom and dad warned me about certain choices I could make in my teen years that would prove to be my undoing. Like many teenagers, I didn't listen! Stubbornly, I insisted on "doing my own thing" rejecting the wisdom of those who cared for me most.

In reading my mom's book, you already know that I've had to learn some very hard lessons. It's very embarrassing to read about the ways I disrespected my parents and strayed from the Lord's best, but perhaps there are those who can benefit from my mistakes. So here are a few things that God has taught me:

- *Parents have your best interests at heart.*
- *Teenagers should listen more to their parents and authorities.*
- *If your folks express reservations about your friends, pay attention!*
- *Education is a valuable tool—get the most out of your academic opportunities.*

- *Being married takes a lot of work, compromise, and maturity.*
- *"Happily ever after" isn't automatic.*
- *It's expensive to add children to your life.*
- *Being frugal pays off! (In other words, don't spend every cent you have in your pocket.)*
- *People have no regrets when they follow God's principles of life.*
- *Honest communication is important in every family.*
- *Unconditional love is the first step in breaking a rebel's heart.*
- *Don't be in too much of a hurry to grow up.*

I'm glad God didn't give up on me and neither did my parents. In fact, through it all, I've learned that I am loved far more than I thought as a teenager! I'm blessed to have not just one, but two sets of parents stand by me, give advice, and encourage me to make wise choices. Now that I'm a mom myself, I see lots of things differently. I'm grateful God has given me a son, and I pray that I'll shower him with the same unconditional love that has been poured out on me. If you know some teenagers headed for trouble, tell them my story. Perhaps they will see that sometimes it's better to stay away from a certain "corn maze" than to enter it and start down a path that will only lead to sorrow.

80

Chapter Thirty-Six

&

Final Thought

I'm so glad God is able to mend and restore broken relationships. My daughter and I have come a long way in the last seven years, but our struggles have not ended. We both have scars on our hearts; nevertheless, we are able to talk more freely about the issues that concern us. God has graced me with a small circle of women who have endured similar situations with their children, and those women have sustained me as we have studied God's Word together.

The Lord is teaching me many lessons. For example, it is easy for me to enumerate Kirsten's sins and to minimize my own.

- She had trouble trusting God.
- She couldn't wait for God's timing.
- She had a high level of anxiety.
- She felt the need to manipulate people and events.
- She lacked self-control.
- She allowed negative thoughts to govern her life.
- She had unrealistic expectations.
- She wanted approval of others.

Now that I look over that list, it seems strangely familiar. It's because those were my sins too. Seeing my sins reproduced in my child was a shock, but God wanted to give me an indelible object lesson. I had no clue how destructive certain patterns were until I experienced their consequences myself.

Kirsten had trouble trusting God's plan for her life. It was difficult for her to see that God had a purpose in placing her in a structured home; she needed boundaries. I struggled with relinquishing my plans and trusting Kirsten's future to God. Now that she had made such irreversible decisions about her life, could God ever turn such chaos into something positive?

Neither one of us wanted to wait for God's timing in our lives. She thought she was ready to make all her own decisions, and I wanted to see some change in Kirsten's heart whether or not she was ready to change. She wanted to grow up too fast, and I wanted answers now. We both wanted to tell God what to do, how to do it, and when.

Kirsten was determined to get her own way, and so was I. Anxiety riddled our souls, and we were both miserable. Our motives were different—she wanted to run away from God, and I wanted her to run to God. However, in the process each one of us was consumed by anxious thoughts.

Both of us wanted to control circumstances for our own purposes. I tried to control her environment, her friends, and her decisions. I thought I knew best. Kirsten also thought if she could just change her environment, her friends, and her decisions, she'd be happy and fulfilled. Both of us tended to forget that God works in the most unusual ways and that sometimes He takes us off the beaten path in order to do a work totally unexpected or unimagined!

Kirsten gave into her passions at the cost of her education. I gave into self-pity and despair at the cost of my sanity and peace. Each of us paid a price in our bodies and spirits because we couldn't get beyond our own selfish desires.

Kirsten became obsessed with all the possessions and freedoms she could not have. Therefore, she could not see how God was at work in her life. I, too, became so focused on all the ways I had been hurt by my child, that I could not immediately see my own sin. Neither one of us was easy to live with, as we too often tried to manage the situation apart from God.

Kirsten wanted perfection as she saw it; so did I. If only she could find her birth parents, she would be happier. It's so amazing that finding her birth parents was extremely beneficial, but it didn't solve her problems. If only she could marry Christopher, life would be fulfilling. I thought if only she would go to a Bible college, get away from certain influences, and take time to grow up, her life would improve. I'm learning to step back and allow God to work in Kirsten's life however He sees fit. At the same time, God is chipping away at me and forcing me to relinquish my own will and follow Him by faith.

Kirsten wanted people to see her as wise and savvy and able to conquer the world. I wanted people to see me as a model parent, one who could calmly handle any situation. I used to have all the answers regarding children, until a prodigal child lived in my home. Both of us had to be humbled. It was a difficult process but enduringly valuable.

My story with Kirsten has served to soften me and make me tender towards proud, stubborn, self-willed people like me. It also has deepened my relationship with God and has forced me to trust Him when the future looked bleak. God isn't limited to using perfect people; obviously He can use anyone, anytime, anywhere, and in any way. I still have much to learn, and there could very well be more surprises in store, but I have a new appreciation for the strength God provides and the peace He sends.

God's Spirit was ministering to me even when all seemed hopeless. I was drawn to His Word to calm my fretting heart. He directed me to specific verses that soothed me. When nothing else could ease my pain, the Lord embedded a piece of eternal truth in my soul. I marked and dated several passages in my Bible, but the one I returned to time and time again was Jeremiah 24:7: "I will give them {Kirsten} a heart to know me, that I am the Lord. They {Kirsten} will be my people, and I will be their God, for they {Kirsten} will return to me with all their heart."

No matter what I knew to be true in my spirit, there were still times when I found myself overcome with grief. I cannot forget how devastating those times were, how I felt like a complete failure, and how there didn't seem to be the slightest hope. That's when my focus was horizontal and not vertical. I wish I could tell you that victory has been won and I now have no problems! Well, the battle isn't over because I am still only one thought away from going back into panic. It is a continual fight to keep my focus on the Lord and His ways and NOT on the circumstances surrounding me.

Kirsten has grown up too. She would tell you she still makes decisions today that I might not wholeheartedly embrace, but at least we enjoy a sweet relationship that is more open and honest than it once was. At the very least, Kirsten knows without a doubt that God loves her too much to allow her to continue in sin. She still faces some consequences from her decisions, and if she had to relive her teen years again, she would live them differently.

We made a deliberate choice to love Christopher too. Our relationship started off on the wrong foot, and we felt quite awkward at the beginning. However, we have come to appreciate his unique qualities, and he will be forever connected to our family. Along our journey together, Christopher's name took on new significance. Literally it means "Christ-bearer," and that's precisely what he became on July 15, 2007 when he was baptized at our home church. We were absolutely thrilled that day as we witnessed that very special step of faith.

Over the course of the next year, life seemed to go relatively well for this couple, but underneath the surface, cracks were beginning to develop in the foundation of their marriage. Our hearts were broken anew as we watched them struggle and eventually sever their relationship. Our hopes, once so filled with promise for a "happy ending," were once again dashed. It was sobering to witness the long-lasting repercussions of poor choices made over the last few years.

All is not lost, however. We are now able to glimpse the mercy and grace of God in Kirsten's life. Because of the path she's walked, she is more humble and open to us. I found it ironic as I listened to myself talking to her about relinquishing her own dreams and trusting the Lord. I was, in fact, passing on to her the same Bible verses, truths, and even "survival tips" I had learned the hard way in my own journey. Those principles had buoyed me in difficult times, and now they would encourage her as well. While the story is far from over, I do have a better spiritual perspective as I continue this new chapter in our lives together. I have experienced God's presence in a profound way, and I know He will be with each one of us.

Today Kirsten and her son live about 2 hours away from us, and we see them often. No one in our family "has it all together," but we have rebuilt our relationship with our eldest child. That in itself seems like a miracle! Steven and I are so grateful we did not reject her when she needed us most. Now, Kirsten calls me several times a week, and we usually end each conversation with "I love you." My, oh my, how our relationship has changed since those darkest days.

Earlier I wrote about how God miraculously, out of everyone in the whole world, placed each of our children in our home. I believe He gave Kirsten to us so that she would be introduced to the Lord Jesus as her Savior, learn the truths of God's Word, and come to know God in a more personal way.

However, Kirsten wasn't the only one who needed to learn something. God used her in our home to teach us too. Now we have a better understanding of forgiveness, unconditional love, and the importance of restored relationships. We've also discovered that relinquishing our timetable, our hopes, our feelings, and our plans was a wise course of action; it was the ONLY way God could bring us back together again. Isn't it wonderful that God knew exactly what each of us needed, even before He joined us as family?

ঙ

Reflection

Looking back I NEVER thought I'd say this, but...there are benefits in having a prodigal child. Steven and I can honestly say TODAY that:

- Our trust in the Lord is deeper.
- Our compassion for others is greater.
- Our willingness to wait on the Lord is longer.
- Our reaction of offering grace and mercy is quicker.
- Our view of God and His purposes is broader.

&

Survival Tip

Be ready to relinquish your own dreams and to embrace all the ways God will work in your life and in your prodigal's life. You won't be sorry.

&

Suggested Bible Study Characters

Joseph

The Woman from Shunem

&

Part Two

&

Bible Studies

Characters arranged in alphabetical order

Cain

&

When You wonder,
"Whatever happened to my perfect life?"

Although the Bible is a Holy Book, it's often surprising to discover that most of the people described therein are not really very holy. The more we study Scripture, the more we realize we operate with many misconceptions. For example:

- God only uses people who have their lives together.
- I'm the only one with a less-than-perfect family.
- Being a faithful parent guarantees that my children will not make poor choices or follow self-destructive ways.

When the unthinkable happens and a child rebels, we are devastated. Most of the parents I personally know sincerely want the best for their children and have committed themselves to rearing them well. When situations turn out poorly, we often blame ourselves unmercifully or ask God WHY He didn't intervene to prevent such a trauma in the family.

It is a productive exercise to evaluate your parenting skills and to take your concerns to God Himself. At the same time, you must realize Satan wants to harden your heart and turn you into a bitter, wounded soul who can never benefit the Kingdom of Heaven. He would rather you doubt the possibility that God is good or that God could ever bring beauty out of the ashes of your situation. (Isaiah 61:3)

No matter how many misconceptions we might have about the way God works, there is one concept that is absolutely clear from Scripture—we all have a sin nature, and its hold on our lives is deceptive and tenacious. The battle is spiritual, and the struggle is enormous. People in rebellion have no idea the danger they have entered, and we who watch them must simply pray and love them. However, the results are not guaranteed. Some hard hearts are eventually softened by the grace of God but regrettably, not all.

1. Read Genesis 2:7-25. As you reflect on the Creation of Adam and Eve, try to imagine what life would be like if you were absolutely perfect in every sense, married to a totally unblemished partner, and living in a pristine environment. Describe such a life. How might it compare or contrast to your life now?

2. The situation changes drastically in Genesis 3. Read this chapter carefully. What is different? Who is at fault? What thoughts might be running through Eve's head as she must deal with a new situation? (Note: She no longer looks at life through the "rosy-colored" glasses of perfection.)

3. Genesis 4 brings a whole new set of complicated circumstances into the lives of Adam and Eve. What are they?

4. In what ways were the two boys different? What is God teaching us about our children as well?

5. What choices did Cain make? How did he respond to God's interaction with him? Who is responsible for his actions?

6. How did he live out the rest of his days? The Bible doesn't give us all the details, but take a guess...do you think he ever turned back to God and his parents? Why?

Well if ever a Bible story chronicled the ugly hold of sin on a life, it is this account. Just think, Adam and Eve were created as PERFECT individuals, schooled in all their knowledge by God Himself. Cain had no bad friends to influence him, no media garbage to purge from his mind. There were no pollutants in the atmosphere to poison his cells. His parents had literally walked with God, and the family genes had truly been perfect at one point in the not-so-distant-past. Nevertheless, the first baby born on earth turned his back on God's best for his life. If rebellion could invade the original family, it shouldn't surprise us that sin can disrupt our families as well.

Satan has a diabolical plan for your life and for your children's lives. The ONLY way we can face the challenge is on our knees, and even then, we have no way of knowing how the story of our children's lives will end. This is a wake-up call. All of us are at risk, and we must NEVER underestimate the power of sin's pull in our lives. Our only hope is the fervent prayer of righteous parents who humbly place their trust in God. What ultimate hope do you find in Romans 16:20?

ಬ If Cain could speak to your heart from the benefit of his experience, what would he say?

so If Adam and Eve could speak to your heart from the benefit of
their experience, what would they say?

so How does this give you strength to face your situation today?

David

ॐ

When the waves of trouble keep rolling in

The young man David is famous for slaying the giant Goliath by depending on the name of the Lord Almighty, the God of the armies of Israel. Read 1 Samuel 17:45. It was such an incredible victory that one might assume the rest of his life would be one success story after another. However, during the next several years, David faced problem after problem after problem. I've endured such a cycle—have you? While many of us might have the strength to deal with one crisis, what should a person do when faced with a long stretch of trouble that seems to have no end?

1. Let's review some of the situations David faced AFTER Goliath. Feel free to browse through the complete story in chapters 18-23 of I Samuel. What problems did David encounter in the following verses?

   • 1 Samuel 18:28-29

   • 1 Samuel 19:10

   • 1 Samuel 20:33

• 1 Samuel 21:10

2. How does David's life resemble yours? How is it different?

3. In what ways does God protect David?

4. Why do you suppose the Lord allowed David to undergo such a time of adversity? Could any good possibly come from it?

5. It is interesting to note that David got himself in worse trouble after he became king and had established peace in the land. How could a time of prosperity be so difficult to handle? (2 Samuel 11)

6. What qualities do you think the Lord wants to teach you during your time of adversity? On the other hand, what types of warnings should you heed during those times when everything seems to be going well?

7. David seemed to thrive spiritually during his time of distress. What is the key to that success? Read 1 Samuel 23:16 and 1 Samuel 30:6b. What do these two verses mean for you?

8. List several specific ways YOU can find strength in the Lord, especially during the worst of days.

9. Psalms 18, 57, 59, and 63 were written by David during this difficult period of his life. What verses/phrases are particularly meaningful to you today? Why? Generally speaking, what is the Lord telling you?

10. Some of the last words Jesus gave His disciples before He went to the cross can soothe our troubled hearts. What comfort do you find in John 16:33?

Be encouraged if you find yourself stuck in crisis after crisis after crisis. God continually protected David while he was running around in the wilderness. He had time to think deeply and penned some of the most comforting words written in Scripture. David's ONLY source of strength was a heavenly One. God also sent a heart-friend to strengthen David's soul and to point him to God. No matter how dismal the circumstances may seem, God is able to bring good out of evil and deepen your roots. Grab onto a friend like David did, and find your strength in God.

∞ If David could speak to your heart from the benefit of his experience, what would he say?

∞ How does this give you strength to face your situation today?

Elijah

❧

When despair overwhelms your soul

I love the story of Snow White, the Handsome Prince, and "happily ever after," but in reality, our earthly life with Jesus will probably NEVER take us to a place where we can just sit and enjoy endless bliss. God loves us too much for that! After all, if we truly could discover an easy spot along life's road and simply coast the final 40 years to Heaven, we'd all be spoiled and selfish. We might even feel so smug that we wouldn't be aware of how much we continually needed God.

So to prevent us from such pride, God often allows obstacles and difficulties to interrupt us and to force us to urgently seek His face. Elijah was a mighty prophet whom God used to display His glory in magnificent and incredible ways. Who could forget him standing against the prophets of Baal on top of Mount Carmel and calling down fire from Heaven? What possibly could go wrong after such a spiritual high?

Read 1 Kings 18:16-46.

1. Describe the situation between Elijah and King Ahab.

2. What character qualities do you see in Elijah as he set out to represent God before the Israelites?

3. If you had been in the crowd that day, what do you think God would have wanted you to remember most?

4. This was an amazing day for God, Elijah, and the people of Israel. As the prophet left the mountain that day, what do you think he might have foreseen for his life and ministry in the next few days?

5. Read 1 Kings 19:1-4. Instead of endless victory and joy, describe how Elijah felt? Under what circumstances have you felt the same?

6. As you review the rest of 1 Kings 19, list the various ways that God made practical provision for His faithful servant. What similar actions can you take that will help you bear your current burden?

7. Like Elijah, it is easy to focus ONLY on a negative perspective. So let's take time to look at the positive side. Write down a list of blessings for which you are thankful in your child's life—for example, good health, safety, family/spiritual heritage, and God's protection. Spend a couple of moments in gratitude to God.

It is comforting to know that one of the mightiest prophets of the Old Testament did not have a cushy life; in fact, he had a surprising problem, a serious bout with depression. (Please note: Depression is NOT just a female complaint!) What Elijah needed was plenty of sleep, angel food cake (mmm), encouragement straight from Heaven, a fresh vision of God Himself, and a ministry partner to help carry the load. The Lord even corrected Elijah's perception that he was all alone. Have you ever felt that way? God wanted Elijah to know that there were not just a handful, but 7,000 others in Israel who stood with him!

God took Elijah's pain and panic personally and took steps to provide for His weary child. He'll do no less for you too. It is easy to fixate on the problems and become overwhelmed with despair; however, if you will lift your eyes to Heaven, you will hear the still small voice of God, and He will provide for you.

ဆ If Elijah could speak to your heart from the benefit of his experience, what would he say?

ဆ How does this give you strength to face your situation today?

Elisha

&

When your eyes need to be opened to a new perspective

Unless you have a child who runs away from home, you do not understand how devastating it can be. From experience, I remember being so overcome by hopelessness that I could scarcely lift my head. The dreadful "D" words—defeat, depression, disillusionment, despondency, discouragement, and disgrace—were often hovering around me.

Looking back, I realize what I needed was a new perspective. There was a dimension to the situation that I had ignored, and God was about to take me on a path I never would have chosen in order to get my attention and deepen my faith!

There is an unforgettable story in the Old Testament that illustrates a similar switch in viewpoints. May it cause you to lift your head and see beyond your "D" words.

Read 2 Kings 6:8-12.

1. There was war between the King of Aram and the King of Israel, but several times God intervened on behalf of Israel through the prophet Elisha (otherwise known as the man of God). What tactic did God use?

2. The King of Aram thought he could outsmart God. What did he do? Read 2 Kings 6:13-14.

3. Put yourself in the servant's shoes; try to describe how the situation appeared to him? Read 2 Kings 6:15.

4. The prophet Elisha, however, had a different perspective. What was it? Read 2 Kings 6:16-17. How does this passage give you a new view about your circumstances?

5. Read the remainder of the story in 2 Kings 6:18-23. What do you see about the character of God as He wins a decisive victory? What can you take from this incident and use for your own encouragement?

The same God Who watched over Elisha and Israel watches over you and your family; therefore, do NOT give in to despair no matter how trapped you feel. Don't ever lose sight of the fact that God is with you and surrounds you with the unseen hosts of Heaven. Ask God to open your eyes so you will see more than the current problems you face. Write out your prayer so you can come back to it again and again and be blessed.

Meditate on Psalm 34:7.

∾ If Elisha could speak to your heart from the benefit of his
experience, what would he say?

∾ How does this give you strength to face your situation today?

$\mathcal{H}$annah

&

When you want answers NOW!

$\int$ometimes we have the idea that heroes of the faith had a simple and easy existence. However, as we study further, we realize they experienced many of the same sorrows and heartaches that we do. Their lives just might seem more carefree to us because their stories are condensed into a few verses or chapters, quickly followed by the outcome. Wouldn't it be easier to endure if we, too, could rapidly skip to the final chapter in our stories? Well, life didn't happen that way for people in Bible times, and it doesn't happen that way for us either. Apparently God has lessons for us to learn in the meantime.

Read Hannah's story recorded in 1 Samuel 1-2:26.

1. Hannah was a woman of great faith who had to live in a tension-filled home. Attempt a guess at how long she had been barren? What emotional issues did she have to overcome? Try to imagine the conversation at their breakfast table. (Perhaps you thought mornings were difficult at your house!)

2. Her husband, while sympathetic, probably didn't fully realize the depth of Hannah's sorrow. What were his actual words? What could he have done or said to ease her pain? What are some words of comfort you could share with someone in her situation?

3. Hannah goes to God with her request and pours out her heart. That's always the best course for us too. Take a moment and write down exactly YOUR heart's desire for your child. Then pray it to God, giving Him the freedom to answer as He sees fit.

4. Of all places, you would expect Hannah to be accepted in the Lord's house; instead, how was she viewed by the high priest, Eli? Have you ever experienced something similar? What is the best way to handle an insensitive attitude or comment?

5. Did God forget Hannah? Read 1 Samuel 1:19. Take comfort in knowing that God has NOT forgotten you either, despite how long you have been waiting for an answer!

6. Describe the "priestly environment" Samuel would be exposed to in Shiloh. How could Hannah leave her little son there? What can you learn from her as you give up your own child into the Hands of God?

7. What vow did she make to the Lord? Did she follow through with it? What do you think was on her heart that final day? Do you think it was easy for Hannah to give up her child? Why or why not?

8. How did God honor Hannah's faith? Read 1 Samuel 2:21.

It's never easy to walk by faith whether you have a prodigal or not. All of us want instant answers, but sometimes God has other lessons for us to learn as we wade through difficult situations. Each of your children is a gift from God; therefore, giving each one back to Him literally or figuratively should set your heart at ease. God is well-aware of your unique situation, and He REMEMBERS you. God is the One Who can bring life to the most barren circumstance and joy to the heaviest soul. You can count on His timing to always be perfect, and His grace will sustain you as you wait.

ဆ If Hannah could speak to your heart from the benefit of her experience, what would she say?

ဆ How does this give you strength to face your situation today?

Jacob

&

When you've lost all hope for your child's future

To be honest, we had some dreadful days as we dealt with the all-encompassing issue of deceit. We had exhausted every avenue of help, and in our distress, there seemed to be no hope. Destructive patterns were dominating our home life, and we wondered if God would ever bring joy to us again. We were dismayed and felt like we were stumbling in the dark.

There is a story of one of the patriarchs from the book of Genesis. If God could remake a character like him and give him a prominent place in His plan, then indeed there is hope for anyone!

1. Read Genesis 25:19-28. What are the various meanings for the name "Jacob"? (You may have to search in footnotes or Bible commentaries.)

2. How would you describe his character as revealed in Genesis 25:27-34?

3. Pretend you are watching as Genesis 27 unfolds before your eyes. Who was the bad influence on Jacob? How many times and in what ways did he mislead his ailing father?

4. Despite the duplicity, what kind of blessing did he receive?

5. Why would God EVER want to use such a flawed character in His eternal plan for mankind?

6. In case you think there were no consequences for Jacob's actions, study Genesis 29:1-30, Genesis 31:38-41, and Genesis 37:12-36. What were they?

7. Eventually God Himself renamed Jacob in Genesis 32:22-30. What is his new name, and what is the significance of it? What lesson do you think God wanted Jacob to learn? What lesson is there for you too?

In Old Testament days, this group of people was commonly referred to as the "Children of Israel" and incredibly today— approximately 5,000 years later—that nation still exists. It is situated on some of the very land God originally promised Jacob. In addition, his descendants were given the privilege of preserving the Old Testament and of becoming the human ancestors of Jesus Christ, Son of God. That's a high calling for one who began so poorly!

If God could restore a conniver like Jacob and give him a prominent place in the Holy Scriptures, then He can certainly remake your situation. Although people may not always escape the consequences of poor choices, God is willing to forgive, offer grace, and make beauty out of our chaos. Reminder: There is always hope where God is at work.

Reflect on Psalm 33:18-22. What is God telling you?

ഇ If Jacob could speak to your heart from the benefit of his experience, what would he say?

ഇ How does this give you strength to face your situation today?

Jehoshaphat

ℰ𝒪

When you don't know what to do

There were moments in my parenting saga when I was completely immobilized because I DID NOT KNOW WHAT TO DO! Some issues are crystal clear. Should children play in the street? NO! Should two-year-olds make all the decisions in the home? NO! Should parents teach their children to love the Lord with all their hearts? ABSOLUTELY! When a teenager, however, makes a series of poor choices and walks out on the spiritual legacy of the family, then how should a parent respond?

We found ourselves all too often unsure of exactly how to proceed. Where should we draw the line? How far should we pursue certain topics? When should we speak up, and when should we clam up? We did not want to push our child away from us permanently because that would eliminate any influence on her life. At the same time, we didn't want our actions to be interpreted as approving sinful choices. We found ourselves in a quandary.

Now what were we to do?

One of the kings of Israel found himself in a similar situation, and his story is a blessing. Perhaps that is just what you need today—a blessing!

1. Read 2 Chronicles 20:1-3. What is the problem for King Jehoshaphat?

2. Where did he go for help? Read 2 Chronicles 20:4-12. (Notice he also had human support; that is something YOU must have.) What elements in his prayer encourage you? Attempt to write a similar prayer tailored for your circumstances.

3. How would you EXPECT God to respond to your prayer in Question 2? In other words what is His perspective of your situation? He sees the end from the beginning, and He is not limited by an earthly viewpoint. Take a moment to write it out.

4. Exactly how did God respond to Jehoshaphat's prayer? Read 2 Chronicles 20:13-17. How are His words comforting to you as well? Even if you do not know exactly how to respond to your child, what CAN you do?

5. Read the account of the actual battle between Jehoshaphat and his enemies in 2 Chronicles 20:18-30. What was the king's role? What was God's role? What was the outcome?

6. Read the previous verses several times. What is God saying directly to your heart and your situation?

I absolutely love that phrase in verse 12: "We do not know what to do, but our eyes are upon YOU." Rather than dwelling on the uncertainty of the moment or the bleakness of the future, we must fix our eyes on the ONLY ONE Who can help, the Lord of all. When you find yourself immobilized, fix your eyes on Him, and may He grant you peace and direction for your journey.

Meditate on Psalm 40. Which verse impacts you? Why?

& If Jehoshaphat could speak to your heart from the benefit of his experience, what would he say?

& How does this give you strength to face your situation today?

Job

&

When you think nothing good could come from your mess

*T*here is a powerful treatise on the topic of suffering in the Bible—the Old Testament book of Job. I never really appreciated it...until I walked my own difficult path. Suddenly it became a lot more interesting.

There are many wonderful truths contained in this book, and I suggest you take the time to read it in its entirety in several translations. I also recommend you attempt an in-depth study. However, for our purposes here, we'll narrow our focus.

1. Read Job 1:1-5. What words from Scripture are used to describe Job? How would you classify him?

2. The story makes a sudden shift to another setting. What is so surprising about the scene in Job 1:6-12?

3. God allows us to watch Satan in action in Job 1:13-19. What does he do? How brutal and cold-hearted are his deeds? What is your conclusion about the relationship of suffering to the diabolical schemes of the devil?

4. How does Job respond to the trauma in his life? If you were in his place, how would you respond? Read Job 1:20-22. What is his perspective? How can you apply these verses to your own situation?

5. Regrettably, Satan isn't finished. Now how does he torment Job? Read Job 2:1-8. It's possible that Satan is adding his devious twists to your suffering too. What perspective can you take to ease your burden?

6. Does Job's wife make it easier or harder for her husband? Why? Read Job 2:9-10. What lesson can we learn from this passage?

7. In the midst of his affliction, Job asks a lot of questions. What are some questions you would like to ask God? What do you think He'd say to you? (See Appendix: Verses of Hope and Healing.)

Several of Job's friends come to visit. Every time I study their words, I become incensed and agree with Job's assessment that they were indeed "miserable comforters." (Job 16:2) I have to wonder, however, what kind of comforter was I in the days before I lived with a prodigal? Did I too freely offer analysis and solutions without fully understanding the depth of pain suffered by a modern-day Job?

8. List some of the comments people have made to you. Were they helpful or hurtful? If you could advise those who wanted to comfort you, what specific words would minister best? What words or phrases should they avoid?

9. One of the treasures of this book is found in Job 23:10. What does this verse tell you about Job's ultimate hope? In what ways does this give you hope too? Find time to personalize this verse, and place it in a prominent place.

Despite his sorrow and pain, Job was adamant—HE WANTED TO HEAR FROM NONE OTHER THAN GOD HIMSELF! He had the courage to ignore some of the potshots of his friends and take his questions and doubts straight to God. Each time I read his story, I feel like a cheerleader yelling: "Go Job, don't quit. You are in a battle for God's reputation. Don't let Satan win this one!" That's when I realize God wants me fighting, ESPECIALLY when the going gets rough.

Finally God speaks. It must have been memorable because Job 38:1 says that He answered Job "out of the storm." The interesting point is, as far as we know, God never let His servant in on the mighty struggle that took place between God and Satan over Job. The only explanation He offers is an unforgettable picture of His sovereignty and creative power. In a nutshell, that is enough for Job. The book ends on a joyful note: "...the Lord made him prosperous again and gave him twice as much as he had before." Job 42:10

10. In your opinion, what was the secret for Job overcoming his situation? How is this truth helpful for you?

No person in his right mind would deliberately choose pain. However, the benefit of extended suffering is that it eventually forces us straight to God. Like Job, we may never have the answers to all our questions, but if we're persistent, we'll catch such an impressive glimpse of the Creator of the universe that our hearts will be at rest. Perhaps God will even use our struggle to put Satan in his place and force him to slither away. When that happens, all glory to God.

Reflect on Psalm 34:18.

ॐ If Job could speak to your heart from the benefit of his experience, what would he say?

ॐ How does this give you strength to face your situation today?

Jonah

ॐ

*When you believe nothing will ever
get your child's attention*

If anyone understood the heart of a runaway, it was God. He hand-selected a man for a job and watched as he proceeded to go in the exact opposite direction. The outcome could have been catastrophic, but God revealed an amazing amount of patience with His servant. Sometimes that's what we need; it may be what our children need as well.

1. Jonah may have thought he was fleeing from an assignment in Nineveh, but according to Jonah 1:3 from Whom was he fleeing? Is that even possible? Read Psalm 139:7.

2. God intervened supernaturally to get Jonah's attention. How? Read Jonah 1:4, 1:17, 4:6, 4:7, 4:8. To what lengths will God go to bring back a runaway?

3. As the ship started tossing and the mariners were getting ready to lighten the ship, what was Jonah doing? Read Jonah 1:5. Perhaps if you could have talked with him at that moment, he might have thought, "Everything is just dandy. It isn't that bad to disobey God!" When have you heard a similar line of reasoning?

4. Read Jonah 1:12-17, and try to imagine the conditions the prophet endured those three days. What kinds of thoughts might have been in his mind?

5. Jonah's actual prayer is recorded in chapter 2. What new insights do you gain about his experience? If the book ended here, what would you predict for the rest of the story?

6. Read chapter 3, and select key phrases that describe the grace of God. God is a God of second chances, and He never gave up on His problem-prophet or a heathen city. How does this perspective encourage you?

7. Now amazingly, the entire city repents—hallelujah! Read chapter 4, and describe Jonah's reaction. How was God's reaction different?

8. The book ends on a somewhat unsettling tone. What do you think God is trying to tell us here? What is your attitude towards people in rebellion? Do you want them punished swiftly, or are you willing to give them a second (and third and fourth) chance?

God sent an amazing revival; however, Jonah was too selfish to enjoy it. Obviously all stories do NOT have happy endings. Nevertheless, God gives every opportunity for people to make the right choice. Instead of zapping Jonah or replacing him, He continued to work with Jonah to bring truth to a heathen nation. God never gave up on Jonah, even when he became "fish vomit" and a pouting evangelist. He won't give up on you or your child either.

ᘒ If Jonah could speak to your heart from the benefit of his experience, what would he say?

ᘒ How does this give you strength to face your situation today?

Joseph

❧

*When it's impossible to imagine that anything good
could come out of your pit*

*G*od sees life from a different perspective than we do. Sometimes we become so focused on our problem that we get an extreme case of tunnel vision. From our vantage point, there is only one solution—OURS!—and only one timetable—NOW! In desperate days, we might not even stop to consider that God could be using the time to work out an outcome far better and far brighter than we could ever imagine. That certainly was the case for one of the patriarchs of the Old Testament.

1. Life started out well for this young man. What advantages did he have? Read Genesis 37:3.

2. Sadly, a happy life did not continue forever. Read Genesis 37:12-28, and retell this incident from Joseph's point of view. Read 42:21 for an additional insight.

3. How might the future have looked to Joseph as he was traveling to Egypt as a slave? What do you imagine he prayed about along the way?

4. Everything seemed to go well in his new occupation. Why? Read Genesis 39:1-6. Before long, however, there was trouble, and Joseph, once again, found himself in a new environment. Read Genesis 39:6-23. Do you think his situation is becoming more hopeless or more hopeful. Why?

5. As Joseph sat in prison for two full years, (Genesis 40-41) what kinds of thoughts do you think he had? Do you think he EVER imagined being named second-in-command to Pharaoh? (God only knows what He has in mind for you or your child.)

6. Comparing Genesis 37:2, Genesis 41:46, and Genesis 41:53-54, approximately how many years was Joseph separated from his brothers? How do you suppose he felt about them as he remembered how they treated him? How would you have felt in his place? How do you feel when your family turns on you?

7. God gives Joseph His eternal perspective in Genesis 50:20. How can you apply this principle to your current situation? (Perhaps it would serve as a good reminder if you copied this verse and taped it some place where you could see it every day.)

God works in unthinkable ways. From a human perspective, He didn't seem to hurry in unveiling the ultimate purpose for Joseph's life. His plan, however, was greater in scope than just getting a boy out of a pit and returning him to his father. Who would have thought that Joseph's trauma would save his entire family? Only GOD would think of such a plan, and He can do the same for you.

∞ If Joseph could speak to your heart from the benefit of his experience, what would he say?

∞ How does this give you strength to face your situation today?

Lazarus, Martha, and Mary

&

When you need to wait a little longer

It's easy to handle a life with a few detours along the way. However, when our entire life goes haywire and we don't know where we're headed, then we can become disoriented and discouraged.

A similar situation happened to a family close to the heart of Jesus. In the midst of their trauma, He gave them an unforgettable lesson about waiting on God and trusting Him for a totally different outcome than they expected.

1. Read John 11:1-3. What was the problem and to whom did the sisters turn for the solution?

2. Try to guess what they may have expected to happen. Instead, what did Jesus say and do? (vs. 4-6) How would you feel if you had observed Jesus in action that day?

3. Even the disciples, personally trained by the Best Teacher ever to walk this earth, seemed unable to grasp what Jesus was about to do. (vs. 7-16) What did Jesus say, and what did the disciples think He meant?

4. What was in Martha's heart as she met Jesus? (vs. 17-24)

5. What was in Mary's heart? (vs. 28-33)

6. Even the crowd gathered there had misgivings about Jesus. How did they feel? How have you felt the same way?

7. Jesus had much more in mind than lowering a fever or curing a stomach ailment. What truths did He intend to reveal to His disciples, His friends, and the onlookers? (vs. 25-27, vs. 38-44)

8. Why did Jesus take the "mysterious" approach in response to the sisters' plea? How has He worked the same way in your situation? What is the benefit to waiting on God?

It's easy to view your situation as it appears without seeing the overall perspective from God's vantage point. It's also natural to become consumed with the enormity of our problems and miss the purpose behind them. We usually want quick solutions and instant answers. Instead, Jesus may want us to wait until our circumstances can ONLY be solved supernaturally and publicly. Then the focus is on Jesus alone, and He's the One Who will receive all the glory. (Who would have thought there would be glory in a cemetery that day???)

So, if you find yourself standing with Mary and Martha who wept as they watched a rapidly deteriorating situation, take heart. God had an unexpected miracle "just around the corner" for them. Imagine the excitement on their faces as they watched Lazarus come out of that tomb! Perhaps one day, YOUR face will have that same expression as God allows you to witness a "resurrection" in your unique circumstances that you never thought possible.

Read Matthew 19:26. What is Jesus saying to you?

∾ If Lazarus, Martha, and Mary could speak to your heart from the benefit of their experience, what would they say?

∾ How does this give you strength to face your situation today?

Mary

ℬ

When your expectations are shattered

As a young mom, it's fun and easy to fantasize about what kind of an adult your child will become. Many of us have big plans and high expectations. When life doesn't unfold according to "our plan," we may resort to self-pity or be tempted to give up.

Recently, I've thought a lot about Mary, mother of Jesus. When she was young, she received the most amazing news the world had ever known, yet her life was not automatically easy. Instead she encountered a series of unexpected detours and dead-ends. No matter how bleak her path may have seemed, God was in control and working out His eternal purposes. The same can be said for me in my struggles…and for you in yours.

1. Read Luke 1:26-38. Mary was a devout Jewish girl who looked forward to the coming of the Messiah. Now an angel appeared and gave her incredible news—she, Mary of Galilee, was to be the Messiah's very own mother! What do you think she imagined for her life and that of her Son in the coming years?

2. Think very carefully about Mary's life. As you read the following passages, put yourself in her shoes, and imagine what she expected to happen at each stage of her life. Then write out those expectations followed by what actually occurred.

a. The birth, Luke 2:1-20.

   • Expectations

   • Reality

b. His childhood, Luke 2:41-52.

   • Expectations

   • Reality

c. The reception by His home church, Luke 4:16-30.

   • Expectations

   • Reality

    d. Mary's place in His adult life, Mark 3:21, 31-35, and John 2:1-11.

       • Expectations

       • Reality

    e. His death, John 19:1-37.

       • Expectations

       • Reality

3. There is no record in Scripture of Jesus revealing Himself to His mother after the resurrection. Do you think she would be upset that the first appearance her son made was to Mary Magdalene? Why or why not?

4. God handed Mary the most incredible assignment—to rear the Savior of the world. Was it easy? Why or why not? Did God clue her in ahead of time to all the twists and turns in her journey? Why or why not? What is God telling you about His ways regarding life on earth?

5. No matter how surprising your life may become, God has promised to be with you. (Hebrews 13:5b) Where have you seen the hand of God in your situation?

6. What do you need to do in order to trust God daily?

I'm sure that as Mary stood at the foot of the cross watching Jesus die, she could not imagine any good that could come from that scene. Although her personal hopes for her Son may have been dashed, God's purposes were fulfilled, and His purposes paid the sin debt of the entire world!

When your expectations are crushed and your life whirls out of control, consider the fact that God is NEVER out of control. He just may be allowing circumstances to achieve a higher purpose than what you had in mind.

ও If Mary could speak to your heart from the benefit of her experience, what would she say?

ও How does this give you strength to face your situation today?

Mary Magdalene

&

When you think you are on a dead-end road

I love the New Testament stories of Jesus interacting with people. Every time, He would cut right to the heart of an issue and then say the most appropriate words. It all seems so simple as we watch Him in action. Sadly, our experiences with our children aren't quite that easy. We often stumble and say the wrong words; in addition, our predicament isn't solved in one short Bible story. Instead it goes on and on and on without any resolution in sight. That's when we become discouraged.

Although our situations may be different from the ones Jesus faced, these stories give us hope. Jesus can take the most improbable person and turn him into a trophy of grace! Don't lose sight of this fact—the power that set people free 2,000 years ago is still available to you today.

Let's meet up close and personal a woman who was very dear to Jesus. Despite the world's depiction of her, she eventually became a grateful believer who followed Him to the very end and beyond.

1. Read Luke 8:1-3. What do you know about Mary Magdalene?

2. Look at the following Biblical accounts of demon possession in Mark 5:1-13 and Mark 9:17-27. What do you think life was like for Mary Magdalene before she encountered Jesus?

3. What words would you use to describe someone who had just been freed from such a devastating life? How do you think she felt about Jesus now? What did she do as a result?

4. The next time she is named in Scripture is at the crucifixion. Put yourself in her place. Would you be there? Why? Read John 19:25. Where was Mary Magdalene? What does that tell you about her commitment to Jesus? What do you think her presence meant to Him? In contrast, where were the disciples? Read Matthew 26:56.

5. Matthew's Gospel gives us additional information. What do you learn about Mary Magdalene in this account? Read Matthew 27:50-61. Why do you think she stayed so long?

6. Read Mark 15:47, 16:1-11, and John 20:1-18. What kinds of emotions can you imagine Mary Magdalene went through that first Easter morning? Was it worth it to see the Lord alive?

7. After His resurrection, of all the people Jesus could have appeared to—Pilate, the chief priests, the soldiers, Peter, His mother—He chose Mary Magdalene. Why?

The scene must have seemed horrific as Mary Magdalene viewed Jesus on the cross. However, God the Father knew the end of the story; He had a plan to provide salvation for the whole world! Can I say the Lord knows the end of your story as well? Put your hope in the miracle-working power of the Resurrected One. If He can take a demon-possessed woman and turn her into a courageous and devoted follower, He can do the same for your child.

๕ If Mary Magdalene could speak to your heart from the benefit of her experience, what would she say?

๕ How does this give you strength to face your situation today?

Moses

&

When you're tempted to say,
"Take me home, Lord. I've had it!"

Isn't it a shock to realize how much disruption one defiant person in your home can cause? As the days drag on and the unpleasantness increases, a parent may begin to entertain some distressing thoughts. Let me assure you, this is not a new phenomenon. Moses, the mighty prophet of old, nearly reached the breaking point. That's when he received some practical advice and comfort from God Himself.

1. Read Numbers 11:1-3. This was not the first time the Israelites complained after God's amazing deliverance from Egypt. Read Exodus 16:2, 17:3. Why was God so angry with them? How did He use Moses?

2. Read Numbers 11:4-9. God had miraculously provided manna for them to eat, but the people weren't exactly thankful. Describe their attitude.

3. How stressful was this situation on Moses, their leader? What specifically did he ask God to do? Read Numbers 11:10-15. (Note: Moses was dealing with about 600,000 military-aged men plus their extended families...not just one teenager! Exodus 12:37) When have you felt the same way? How do you believe God wants you to respond to your trials?

4. What practical step did God first take to relieve the burden for Moses? Read Numbers 11:16-17. What does this mean for you?

5. Again, God isn't particularly pleased with the complaining spirit of the Israelites. How do you know? Why do you think griping is so odious to the Lord? Read Numbers 11:18-20.

6. Moses became very discouraged as he stared at the enormity of the problem. Instead, God had a different view—what was it? Read Numbers 11:21-23. What is God saying to you too?

7. Providing meat for a whole nation was an easy task for God. Read Numbers 11:31-32. What part of your situation is easy for God to solve? Can you trust Him?

Sometimes God gives us a difficult assignment, like to lead a group of stubborn Israelites through the desert or to love a teenager who is bound and determined to get his own way. In those times, resist the urge to quit, complain, or withdraw. Like Moses, surround yourself with Spirit-directed people who will help you carry the burden, and recall that the Lord's arm is NOT too short to solve any dilemma.

ℂ If Moses could speak to your heart from the benefit of his experience, what would he say?

ℂ How does this give you strength to face your situation today?

Paul and Silas

&

When you don't feel like singing

*P*ain is NOT fun—whether it's physical, emotional, financial, relational, or any other type you can imagine. The natural responses to pain include crying, sighing, withdrawing, blaming, and doubting.

It usually doesn't occur to us, however, to sing joyfully to God in the MIDST of our problems. Two prisoners featured in the book of Acts are a wonderful example of joy despite the circumstances.

1. Paul and Silas traveled to Philippi. What did they do that got them in so much trouble? Read Acts 16:16-19.

2. Describe the accusations, the justice system, and the punishment they received. Read Acts 16:20-24.

3. How would you feel if you had been in their place? (Would you be looking for a hymnbook?) What would you expect for your future? How would you pray specifically?

4. How did Paul and Silas spend their evening? What were the results? Read Acts 16:25-34.

5. What kind of an impression do you think these two men made on the magistrates and officers? Read Acts 16:35-39.

6. Read Acts 16:40. When it was over, how do you think Paul and Silas encouraged the people at Lydia's house? What comments would have been most helpful to them?

7. What could possibly be the purpose of singing in the midst of trauma?

God created us as emotional beings, and sometimes when we are distraught, music can raise our spirits. (1 Samuel 16:23) Make every effort to listen to good Christian music, and filter every thought that comes your way. People who are overcome with grief don't need to hear messages of gloom and doom. Concentrate only on things that are true, noble, right, pure, lovely, and admirable. (Philippians 4:8) If you catch a vision of Who Jesus is, your pain and problems will feel infinitely smaller. Now that's a reason to sing!

8. Make a list of songs you can sing the next time you are overwhelmed with pain. Record in the space below the blessings or insights you receive.

9. Take some time now to worship the Lord with songs of praise. Perhaps there will be no earthquake to release you from "your prison," but lift up your eyes to Jesus and His mighty power, and your problems on earth won't seem so overwhelming.

ଓ If Paul and Silas could speak to your heart from the benefit of their experience, what would they say?

ଓ How does this give you strength to face your situation today?

Peter

&

When you worry that there is nothing worse than denying the Lord

I imagine every parent realizes sooner or later, that their children will make mistakes, but some mistakes carry serious consequences. The very LAST behavior parents would ever want from their children is to reject their spiritual heritage. What could be worse than denying the Lord?

It's interesting that Jesus dealt with a similar issue. He prayerfully selected 12 men to be His disciples. However, one of them proved to be a traitor, and another denied even knowing Him. The most prominent of this group was a man named Peter who all too often acted just like a teenager—he asked a lot of questions, he spoke without thinking, he was impulsive, self-centered, and didn't listen well to his Teacher. The worst moment came the evening before the crucifixion.

1. Read Matthew 26:31-35. What was happening? In your own words, tell what Jesus predicted. How did Peter (and the other disciples) respond?

2. Jesus knew what was about to happen that night. What DIDN'T He say to Peter? What does this tell you about the ways of God?

3. Read Luke 22:54-60. What were Peter's exact words? How could he make such a statement? How have your child's actions or words betrayed you, your family, or your faith? Why do you think betrayal hurts so badly?

4. Sometimes it's so easy to focus on the sins of our children that we forget our own! When have you ever denied the Lord in any way? How did it make God feel? What are some steps YOU can take to make your relationship right with the Lord? How does God want you to react to your child?

5. Read Luke 22:61-62. Describe the look you imagine Jesus gave Peter. Did He say anything? What would be the worst part of this situation for Peter?

6. How do you think Peter spent the next several hours? If he could have prepared a speech to give Jesus that night, what do you think he would have said?

7. In Mark's account of the resurrection, what is so precious about the words of the angel (the man in the white robe) to the women at the tomb? Read Mark 16:6-7. What does this tell you about the heart of God?

8. In John 21:15-19, Peter and Jesus have a little chat. What is so remarkable about this conversation? What is the main message Jesus wants to communicate to His disciple? Do you think Peter is really listening this time? Why?

9. Peter becomes a powerful preacher from that day forward. (If you want an example, read Acts 2:14-41.) There would be no more denying the Lord. To what do you attribute this reversal? What can you learn from Jesus in dealing with a person who has walked away from his faith?

It is inconceivable that one of Jesus' closest friends on earth could have denied Him at precisely the time he was needed most. Remember, Peter had a lot of advantages:

- He was taught by the World's Greatest Teacher.
- He personally witnessed many miracles.
- He had been given authority to heal and cast out demons.
- He had walked on water.
- He was present at the Transfiguration and got a glimpse of Jesus in His glory (Matthew 17:1-13).

NEVERTHELESS, he still denied the Lord, even after being forewarned by the Son of God Himself. If Peter could be so enticed to betray his faith, how much more susceptible are today's teenagers?

The main point is not to excuse behavior but to learn from Jesus about how to deal with serious sins. PLEASE NOTICE THAT JESUS RESTRAINED HIS WORDS AND REJECTED THE IDEA OF GIVING PETER A LONG DISSERTATION ON REBELLION! In addition, He did NOT abandon Peter, instead He sought to maintain a relationship with His wayward disciple. (Jesus KNEW the future. Because we don't, we are forced to trust

God Who causes our faith to grow.) Your teenager needs the same view of Christ on the cross that Peter saw. Perhaps then, his heart will break and he'll be on the road to recovery. Who knows, the next evangelist of the century just might live at your house. God wants to restore people—do you?

ℰ𝒪 If Peter could speak to your heart from the benefit of his experience, what would he say?

ℰ𝒪 How does this give you strength to face your situation today?

Rahab

❦

When you feel your child is too far away to ever become a member of God's family

There is a surprising hero in one Old Testament story. She's a woman who might raise some eyebrows if she strolled into our churches today, but God looked beyond her sin and circumstances and welcomed her into His family. I trust you'll remember her story when you are tempted to think that after all that's transpired, your child could NEVER be a part of the family of God.

1. The children of Israel were ready to take possession of the Promised Land. Led by Joshua, the people had to overcome the first obstacle—the walled city of Jericho. Where did the spies go? Why would they end up there? Read Joshua 2:1.

2. As we are introduced to Rahab, we see that she is a most unlikely hero. What strikes does she have against her? Read Joshua 2:1-7.

3. No matter her occupation, her nationality, or her character, Rahab was about to become a tool in the hand of the Lord. What did she know about the God of Israel? Read Joshua 2:8-13. What facts do you know about God that will give you confidence to act in the days to come?

4. Read Joshua 2:14-21. What was the agreement? What was the sign?

5. Read the actual account of the battle in Joshua 6:1-21. Who deserves credit for the victory? Why?

6. Did Joshua and the spies keep their word to a heathen prostitute? Read Joshua 6:22-23. Where was she taken? Why?

7. What difference do you notice in Joshua 6:24-25? What did it mean for Rahab? What does it mean for your prodigal?

8. There are two very precious passages of Scripture in the New Testament related to Rahab. One is in Hebrews 11, commonly called the Hall of Faith. Skim through that chapter, and list some of the heroes mentioned there. Whom do you discover included in verse 31? What is the key to her turnaround? What is the message for us?

9. The second passage is Matthew 1:1-16 which lists the human genealogy of Jesus Christ, the Son of God. What kinds of people would you expect to be included in such a prestigious position? Who is included in verse 5? What does that tell you about the grace of God?

If a Canaanite "woman of the night" could become a literal part of the family of God, then your prodigal cannot be too far gone to be considered for a heavenly rescue—no matter how scarlet his sins might be. My prayer is that your child will eventually be found AMONG the people of God and be a candidate for induction into this century's Hall of Faith. "With God all things are possible." Matthew 19:26

𝄢 If Rahab could speak to your heart from the benefit of her experience, what would she say?

𝄢 How does this give you strength to face your situation today?

Samson

ℰ

When you feel like giving up

When kids are little, their mistakes are relatively minor, but as they grow towards adulthood, their miscues cause far graver consequences. To make matters worse, some people seem to get stuck in a downward cycle of poor choices until their lives careen completely out of control. Such a life path can be extraordinarily painful to watch, and we as parents can become so distraught, that we begin to wonder if even God could save our children from themselves!

I've often wondered how the mother of one famous Old Testament character dealt with the poor choices and the unexpected death of her son. Her journey might sound familiar to you.

1. Read Judges 13:1-5. Describe the situation for the nation of Israel. What details do we learn about Mrs. Manoah?

2. If you had been barren and the Angel of the Lord appeared to you with such a message, how carefully would YOU follow His instructions? At that point, how do you think this lady envisioned the future ministry of her son?

3. How serious was this couple about parenting the miracle-child? Read Judges 13:8-24.

4. All too soon, Samson begins to make choices that go against the Law of Moses and his parents' wishes. Read Judges 14-16:22, and make a list of his unwise or sinful decisions.

5. How would you evaluate this "deliverer" of Israel by his actions? If his mother came to you blaming herself for his poor choices, what would you say?

6. How did Samson die? Read Judges 16:23-31. How does this ending contrast with your answer in Question 2b?

7. What startling insight can you gain from Judges 14:4 and Hebrews 11:32? How could you apply this principle to your own difficulty?

8. We aren't told whether or not Mrs. Manoah lived long enough to see the final days of her son. If so, what words might describe her feelings on the day of his burial?

9. Did God accomplish His purpose in the life of Samson as foretold by the Angel of the Lord? Read Judges 13:5. Did it happen the way you or I might have expected it? What is God telling you?

Samson's mom had every reason to be heartbroken over the actions of her son, and obviously this story did not have a warm, comfy ending. Nevertheless, God preserved it for us. Through it we are reminded of some very important lessons:

- No parent (even an angel-taught one) has perfect children.
- Children who insist on sinning must pay the consequences sooner or later.
- God can use even the sin of man to accomplish His purposes.
- If Samson could eventually be included among the heroes of the Bible, perhaps there will be a place reserved for your child there too.

While people might be tempted to give up on others, God NEVER does. So if you want to be like God, DON'T EVER GIVE UP ON YOUR CHILDREN!

℘ If Samson could speak to your heart from the benefit of his experience, what would he say?

℘ How does this give you strength to face your situation today?

Shadrach, Meshach, and Abednego

ℰℴ

When you don't know where your child is

It is very scary to lose sight of your children. Perhaps some of you have a memory of being at the mall and suddenly missing a little child. Most of us become immediately panicked as we remember kidnapping stories on television. It might be less than 60 seconds before we are reunited, but the interval seems very, very long.

As our children grow up, we come to realize those times of continual contact and quick conformity to our standards don't always happen. Some kids prove to be quite daring, defiant, and determined to get away from us. In those times we learn most vividly that although our children are out of our sight, they are NEVER out of God's sight.

We don't know anything about the parents of Daniel's three friends, but I imagine they were horrified as their sons were kidnapped and carried off to Babylon several hundred miles away. What would happen to them? Would they forsake their faith? How could God ever allow such a tragedy?

Whatever choices resulted in your child's present predicament, remember, it is the same God Who watches over all. Perhaps it will be "in the fire" that your son or daughter will be delivered too.

1. Read Daniel 1:1-7. What kinds of young people did Nebuchadnezzar take? What do you imagine they thought would happen to them as they started off on this long journey?

2. Read Daniel 1:8-20. What was their first test, and how well did they do? What do you think was the secret of their success? What is God saying to you too?

3. The next test for these boys who were so far away from home is much, much more difficult. What were their choices? Read Daniel 3:1-6.

4. How conspicuous were Shadrach, Meshach, and Abednego in their rebellion to the king's decree? How did Nebuchadnezzar find out, and what was his reaction? Read Daniel 3:8-15.

5. Many young people would have caved in to the pressure, but God was good in allowing these three to be together. How would you evaluate their faith as they stand before the king? Read Daniel 3:16-18. How does it compare to your faith in dealing with your current circumstances?

6. Who won the battle between God and Nebuchadnezzar, the mightiest king on earth? Read Daniel 3:19-27. What blessing do you discover in verse 25? What does it mean for you?

7. What truths do you discover about God and these young men in Daniel 3:28-30? How do they encourage you with your child?

God saved these young men in impossible circumstances. They were a long way from home and beyond the godly influences of their parents. They were pressured to deny their faith and were literally put through a fiery ordeal. However, the Holy One of Israel did not leave them alone; He walked right beside them and rescued them.

I can't promise a miraculous ending to your story like this one, but I can promise that the Lord Himself will walk with YOU through your fire. (Isaiah 43:2) No other God can save like our God—won't you trust Him?

❧ If Shadrach, Meshach, and Abednego could speak to your heart from the benefit of their experience, what would they say?

❧ How does this give you strength to face your situation today?

The Disciples

❧

When it seems like Jesus is unaware of the depth of your struggles

*J*esus was on a mission to train His disciples so that they would continue His work after He returned to Heaven. The question is—what's the best way to accomplish such a goal? He knew those 12 men very well; they would learn far better from a hands-on experience than from reading articles or listening to wonderful instructions. One day He decided to take them on a little boat ride across the Sea of Galilee.

1. Read Mark 4:35-37. Whose idea was it to get into the boat? What happened? Do you think Jesus was "caught by surprise"? Why or why not? Use your imagination; what was this boat ride like?

2. Read Mark 4:38. Where was Jesus? How could He appear to be so oblivious to the danger?

3. Do you imagine those 12 men tried to take care of the situation themselves before involving Jesus? Describe a time when you also have done something similar.

4. What question did the disciples ask Jesus? Describe a time when you felt the same way—Jesus was in "your boat" but a storm was raging and He didn't seem to care.

5. Did Jesus care about the disciples and whether or not they would drown? How do you know? Does Jesus care about you in your situation? How do you know?

6. Try to imagine the scene recorded in Mark 4:39. Describe Jesus—His face, His body language, and His actions. What kinds of looks were on the disciples' faces? What types of thoughts were rolling around inside their heads? Also read verse 41. Try your hand at being an artist. Draw this scene using stick figures and dialogue.

7. Jesus spoke several short phrases or thoughts. Read Mark 4:39-40. List each one below. How might Jesus be saying the same things to you in the midst of your storm? (Note: Some translations record three separate thoughts; some record four.)

8. Read Mark 4:41. Why do you think the disciples were terrified after the storm was calmed? Why would they ask, "Who is this?" Didn't they already know? What impressed them the most in this situation?

9. Why didn't Jesus tell His disciples ahead of time about His intentions? What could possibly be the benefit of being thrown out into a storm without warning—both for the disciples and for you?

Although Jesus promises not to forsake you, He never guarantees a peaceful, easy trip through life even if He IS living in "your boat." In fact, it's only in the storms that we come to see His incredible power. My prayer is that the next time you have the opportunity to see the winds or the waves in action, you will remember Who it is that controls them.

He is the One Who cares for you. He is the One Who will see you through.

✌ If the disciples could speak to your heart from the benefit of their experience, what would they say?

✌ How does this give you strength to face your situation today?

The Man Born Blind

❧

When you just want to know "Why?"

One question that really bothered us over the course of our journey was WHY? Even Jesus Himself asked the same question: "My God, My God, WHY have You forsaken me?" (Mark 15:34b) We analyzed our methods and our actions; we relived every event, and we basically drove ourselves crazy trying to understand WHY such betrayal could happen in our family. To us, it made no sense at all, and that conclusion was most disturbing.

The disciples came to Jesus one day with a similar question, and Jesus gave them a surprising answer.

1. Read John 9:1-3. In your own words, write out the question of the disciples and the answer of Jesus. What does He mean?

2. Jesus then proceeded to fix this man's problem. What did he do? Read John 9:6-7. (It seems like a strange way to heal, but Jesus is NEVER bound by what seems like the best solution to us!)

3. Study the remainder of the story in John 9:8-41. What is so precious about the response of the man born blind?

4. What is so alarming about the response of his parents?

5. What is so maddening about the response of the Pharisees? What important truth were they missing because of their narrow focus?

6. For whom do you feel more sorry—the Pharisees or the man? Why?

7. Go back and reread the account of this incident. This time look at it through the eyes of Jesus. How did He orchestrate the details so that the work of God would be displayed?

8. Specifically what was He demonstrating for His disciples?

9. What was His ultimate purpose for the man born blind?

Let's pretend YOU are this man and are now being interviewed for the evening newscast. What would you say to a reporter's questions about the issue of blindness and the power of Jesus? Write out the dialogue below.

God works in the most mysterious of ways. (Isaiah 55:9) He is the only One Who can bring:

- Good out of evil (Genesis 50:20)
- Beauty out of ashes (Isaiah 61:3)
- Victory out of death (1 Corinthians 15:55)
- Light out of darkness (2 Corinthians 4:6)

Jesus came to earth as a man in order to satisfy God's penalty for our sins. Why was He forsaken at the cross? —to achieve His mission and to secure salvation for us. Hallelujah! The specific answer to your "why" questions will be different, but in those times, focus your energy on WHO Jesus is and WHY He came to earth. After your eyes are opened to the impact of His amazing love, you will be strengthened as you wait for His answers about your particular situation. Your story with your prodigal isn't finished yet, and only God knows the final ending.

Reflect on Romans 8:28-39.

≈ If the man born blind could speak to your heart from the benefit of his experience, what would he say?

≈ How does this give you strength to face your situation today?

The Prodigal Son

&

When your child demands his own way

*I*n Luke 15, Jesus tells three parables, all of which revolve around the search for something lost. While no parent ever wants to consider the possibility that a child could be lost by leaving home prematurely, it can happen. How in the world is a parent supposed to feel, and what is he to do? Let's see what Jesus says.

Read Luke 15.

1. What elements do the three parables have in common?

2. How are they different?

3. What principle is Jesus teaching the Pharisees? What principle do you believe He has in mind for us?

4. Make a list of the poor choices the younger son made. How do they compare to the choices you or your child have made?

5. What is the turning point in the story of the prodigal son? Who ultimately orchestrates the problems that cause him to remember home? What do you think it might take to get your child to long for home again?

6. How would you describe the father's actions, both when the son left and when he returned? What didn't he do? In what ways does he remind you of Jesus? How can you follow the example of both the father and Jesus?

7. What was the root cause of the older brother's anger? Is there someone in your family with a similar view? If so, how can you use verses 31 and 32 to respond like the father in this story?

The father in this story was originally put in a very awkward position. The situation had gotten so desperate that when the young son demanded his own way, the father decided to grant his request. Can you relate to the pain the dad felt as his boy walked away? However, the story isn't over. As the prodigal experienced the consequences of his choice, his heart was humbled, and he began thinking of home. What does Psalm 106:15 say regarding this?

There may come a time when your child will demand his own way too. While he might seem "lost" to you, remember he is never out of God's sight. Perhaps the selfishness of your prodigal will be what God will use to crush his heart and to make him consider coming home.

In some ways it's comforting to remember that Jesus knows that children and adults will make mistakes—even some with horrible and far-reaching effects. BUT, that's why He came to earth—to annihilate our sins and to offer us a place in His family. (Matthew 9:12-13, Luke 19:10)

If Jesus can welcome sinners into His home, surely we can too. Instead of rehearsing the past and all the struggles you've endured, contemplate the moment your child "comes to his senses" and returns home. May these words be heard at your house too: "For this son of mine was dead and is alive again; he was lost and is found." (Luke 15:24a) Now that's a reason for a party!

ᛰ If the prodigal son could speak to your heart from the benefit of his experience, what would he say?

ᛰ If the father could speak to your heart from the benefit of his experience, what would he say?

ᛰ How does this give you strength to face your situation today?

The Widow of Nain

%

When you think nobody cares

*E*ven a sunny day seems dreary when your child is in trouble. There are times when you feel that no one knows and that no one even cares about the extent of your grief. To make matters worse, even if someone did feel your pain, what could he do about it? I'm sure that's exactly how a woman from the town of Nain felt 2,000 years ago. The Bible doesn't give us all the details we'd like to know, but let's use our "sanctified imagination" and see what we can learn from her story.

1. Read Luke 7:11-17. Her specific circumstances might be different from yours, but she understood what it meant to have her dreams dashed. How does it feel?

2. What kinds of emotions and thoughts do you think she struggled with that day?

3. If you were to miraculously transport her to your town and time, what resources would be available to her? However, in her day, how did the future look for a childless widow?

4. For the funeral procession, there was a large crowd with her, but ordinarily, what happens to all those people in the ensuing days, weeks, months, years?

5. She might have felt all alone, but there was Someone Who noticed her. Who? How did He feel, and what were the first two words He said to her?

6. Since she did not know how her story would end, how might she have responded when Jesus said, "Don't cry."

7. What incredible miracle did Jesus perform just for this one very sad mom? Describe Jesus giving her son back to her.

8. Now what types of emotions filled her heart? If she could control herself enough to speak, what would she say to Jesus? If God would miraculously intervene and give your child back to you today, how would YOU react?

I love the testimony of the people that day: "God has come to help his people." This is just as true today as it was then. We just don't know when, where, or how. One fact IS certain, however—God knows all about our circumstances, and His heart goes out to us too. He may not literally raise the dead in your case, but I know He can bring life and hope to you, no matter how impossible your journey seems.

Never, never, never give into despair because on a day you least expect it, Jesus could very well turn your wailing into dancing. (Psalm 30:11-12)

❧ If this dear woman from the town of Nain could speak to your heart from the benefit of her experience, what would she say?

❧ How does this give you strength to face your situation today?

The Woman at the Well

☙

When you wonder if your child has made so many mistakes,
he could never be used by God

When your children make a series of poor choices, you often wonder what will become of them. Would God EVER be able to use someone with such a past? In a word, the answer is YES! The more I've studied Scripture and the more I've learned about the ways of Jesus, the more convinced I am that God can use anyone, any time, anywhere!

Jesus created a lot of controversy when He lived on earth, and the ones who gave Him the most grief were the religious leaders of the day. He simply didn't act the way they thought He should. In fact, you might also find out that some of your friends won't agree with your approach to your prodigal either. Be sure to follow the leading of the Holy Spirit, and do what HE asks you to do.

Rather than giving up on people, Jesus found ways to motivate, encourage, and use some of the most surprising characters. In one remarkable incident, He used a woman who was up to her eyeballs in sin to bring the good news of salvation to an entire city. (Imagine her joining your door-to-door evangelism team.)

Read her story in John 4:1-42.

1. Where was Samaria, and how did the Jewish people feel about its inhabitants?

2. How did Jesus cross paths with this woman? Do you think it was an accidental meeting or an intentional one? Why?

3. A most unusual conversation takes place. What is Jesus' purpose? How does this woman miss the main point?

4. Describe her marital status. How would people in Jesus' day have viewed such a situation? How did the disciples view her in vs. 27? How have others treated your prodigal? In contrast, how did Jesus treat this woman at the well?

5. Did Jesus give her a long dissertation on the severity of her sins? Why? Did He wait until she had taken an extended course on evangelism before He used her? Why?

6. What words would you use to describe her actions when she went back to town? What was the response?

7. Literally, where was the harvest for souls most ripe? Who was the sower, and who was the reaper?

8. Why did Jesus use a woman with a very tarnished reputation to advance the Kingdom of God?

Satan wants you to waste precious time worrying that your child's sin will disqualify you or him from ever being useful to God. However, I'm learning that some of the most glorious trophies of God's grace have walked the most crooked paths. Who knows how God will use your personal story with your child in the lives of other people. Perhaps it will be this testimony about the grace of God that will eventually lead many people to Jesus.

๛ If the woman from Samaria could speak to your heart from the benefit of her experience, what would she say?

๛ How does this give you strength to face your situation today?

The Woman from Shunem

&

When you think you could never say, "All is well."

*A*ll of us will face difficult and puzzling circumstances, but it is in those trying times that our faith grows the most. We are going to meet a dear woman from the Old Testament who was just minding her own business, when one day her life was changed forever! In the midst of her trauma, she intentionally committed her child to the Lord. May her example inspire you to do the same.

1. How did God bring the prophet Elisha into this lady's life? Read 2 Kings 4:8-10. What characteristics do you see in her?

2. How did Elisha decide to repay her? (Note: She didn't ask; nevertheless, God knew the desires of her heart. He also knows yours!) Read 2 Kings 4:11-16. Why was her initial response "No"? What was she thinking?

3. Approximately one year later, as recorded in 2 Kings 4:17, this lady gave birth to a son. What kinds of thoughts would fill her heart and mind as she looked at this child? How would she feel towards God and Elisha?

4. When the unthinkable happened, how did she handle the situation? What was her main priority, and what were the first words out of her mouth? Read 2 Kings 4:18-23. How does her response compare to your response when the unthinkable happens to your child?

5. The King James Version translates her words as "It shall be well." How could she make such a comment? Why didn't she tell her husband their son had died?

6. Elisha described her as being in "bitter distress." (vs. 27) Describe a time when you have felt the same way about your child.

7. This woman was on a mission, and she would let nothing stop her from going directly to Elisha. How did he respond, and what happened? Read 2 Kings 4:24-35.

8. Read 2 Kings 4:36-37, and rewrite it from the Shunammite's perspective.

This is a true story recorded for us in the pages of the Bible. It's comforting to know that other women have gone through difficult trials, and some of the issues they faced were serious and life-threatening. It's also encouraging to realize it IS possible to utter the words "It is well" BEFORE a mother witnesses the answer to her prayers. There can be peace and not panic in the midst of trouble.

I can't begin to imagine how God will work in the life of you and your child, but I do know God cares deeply about each crisis we endure. Moreover, He wants us to run to Him for hope and help, letting nothing stop us from our mission. May you have the deep faith of this woman from Shunem, and may God say to you one day, "Here is your child, take him home."

ಬಿ If this woman from Shunem could speak to your heart from the benefit of her experience, what would she say?

ಬಿ How does this give you strength to face your situation today?

The Woman Taken in Adultery

ℬ

When you don't feel like offering grace

The question often arises, "How does a parent treat a child still stuck in rebellion?" An accompanying question is, "How does a parent treat friends of the prodigal who may be responsible for that rebellion?" This can be a difficult dilemma and one that may even be controversial. We wrestled over and over with this issue because there were times we were tempted to be short on patience and quick to judge. Eventually we had to ask ourselves, "How would that course of action EVER point our child to the Lord or motivate her to come back to our family?" I took a fresh look at the life of Jesus and found an irresistible example.

There were people in Jesus' day who had a hard time believing He was the Messiah. From their viewpoint, He was soft on sin and didn't adhere to their version of the Law. Apparently they didn't understand the power of grace.

1. Read Matthew 9:9-13. This passage demonstrates how the Pharisees viewed Jesus interacting with "sinners." What were they most concerned about? On the other hand, what was Jesus concerned about?

2. Read John 8:1-11 where we see Jesus teaching all the people. Try to imagine the scene. Where was He? Describe the interruption.

3. What was the ulterior motive of the Pharisees? Did they succeed or not? Why?

4. I've always wanted to ask this group of men a couple of questions. For example, how does one discover someone "in the very act," and where was the offending male? Do you have any other questions?

5. Put yourself in the place of this publicly disgraced woman. How would you feel? What would you expect to hear from the Jewish Rabbi teaching in the temple courts?

6. Describe the way Jesus treated her. How does it contrast with the way of the Pharisees? Which approach would better motivate her to leave her life of sin? Why?

7. As the woman walked away that day, what kinds of thoughts were in her head? Imagine this lady coming to your church and giving her testimony. What would she say about Jesus and His grace?

8. There is another instance where Jesus surprises us with His actions. Read John 13:1-11. It is a poignant scene in the Upper Room as Jesus is preparing to die for all the sinners in the world. He washes the feet of every disciple including Judas? How much grace would it take to perform such an act? How does Jesus want you to act toward those who have wronged you?

9. As Jesus is arrested in the garden, He comes face to face with His betrayer. What is so startling about the words of Jesus? Read Matthew 26:47-50. What does it mean for you?

10. Jesus came on a mission to earth. What was His purpose? Read Luke 19:10. What is your purpose?

Grace means granting favor to someone who is undeserving. It is a wonderful theological principle to discuss, but it is an entirely different matter to live it out on a day-to-day basis. If the Holy Sinless Son of God could offer grace to sinners, can we do the same for the people God has placed within our realm of influence? May your answer be YES, by the grace of God.

Reflect on Psalm 103:10.

ຂ   If this woman could speak to your heart from the benefit of her experience, what would she say?

ຂ   How does this give you strength to face your situation today?

Appendix

❧

Verses of Hope and Healing

*T*here is nothing like the soothing words of Scripture on a broken heart. Here are some of the verses that lifted my heart when nothing else could. May you return to them over and over again and claim the promises of God. ❧

Is anything too hard for the LORD?

Genesis 18:14a

The LORD turn his face toward you and give you peace.

Numbers 6:26

Have I not commanded you?
Be strong and courageous.
Do not be terrified;
do not be discouraged,
for the LORD your God will be with you wherever you go.

Joshua 1:9

You are my lamp, O LORD;
the LORD turns my darkness into light.

2 Samuel 22:29

Look to the LORD and his strength;
seek his face always.

1 Chronicles 16:11

Do not grieve,
for the joy of the LORD is your strength.

Nehemiah 8:10b

But he knows the way that I take;
when he has tested me, I will come forth as gold.

Job 23:10

God's voice thunders in marvelous ways;
he does great things beyond our understanding.

Job 37:5

The LORD is a refuge for the oppressed,
a stronghold in times of trouble.

Psalm 9:9

You are my hiding place;
you will protect me from trouble
and surround me with songs of deliverance.

Psalm 32:7

I sought the LORD, and he answered me;
he delivered me from all my fears.

Psalm 34:4

The righteous cry out, and the LORD hears them;
he delivers them from all their troubles.
The LORD is close to the brokenhearted
and saves those who are crushed in spirit.
A righteous man may have many troubles,
but the LORD delivers him from them all.

Psalm 34:17–19

God is our refuge and strength,
an ever-present help in trouble.

Psalm 46:1

Cast your cares on the LORD
and he will sustain you;
he will never let the righteous fall.

Psalm 55:22

When I am afraid, I will trust in you.

Psalm 56:3

My flesh and my heart may fail,
but God is the strength of my heart
and my portion forever.

Psalm 73:26

In the day of my trouble I will call to you,
for you will answer me.

Psalm 86:7

He heals the brokenhearted
and binds up their wounds.

Psalm 147:3

Hope deferred makes the heart sick,
but a longing fulfilled is a tree of life.

Proverbs 13:12

Commit to the LORD whatever you do,
and your plans will succeed.

Proverbs 16:3

The name of the LORD is a strong tower;
the righteous run to it and are safe.

Proverbs 18:10

You will keep in perfect peace
him whose mind is steadfast,
because he trusts in you.
Trust in the LORD forever,
for the LORD, the LORD, is the Rock eternal.

Isaiah 26:3–4

Do you not know?
Have you not heard?
The LORD is the everlasting God,
the Creator of the ends of the earth.
He will not grow tired or weary,
and his understanding no one can fathom.
He gives strength to the weary
and increases the power of the weak.
Even youths grow tired and weary,
and young men stumble and fall;
but those who hope in the LORD
will renew their strength.
They will soar on wings like eagles;
they will run and not grow weary,
they will walk and not be faint.

Isaiah 40:28–31

So do not fear, for I am with you;
do not be dismayed, for I am your God.
I will strengthen you and help you;
I will uphold you with my righteous right hand.

Isaiah 41:10

For I am the LORD, your God,
who takes hold of your right hand and says to you,
Do not fear; I will help you.

Isaiah 41:13

When you pass through the waters,
I will be with you;
and when you pass through the rivers,
they will not sweep over you.
When you walk through the fire,
you will not be burned;
the flames will not set you ablaze.

Isaiah 43:2

Forget the former things;
do not dwell on the past.
See, I am doing a new thing!
Now it springs up; do you not perceive it?
I am making a way in the desert
and streams in the wasteland.

Isaiah 43:18-19

I will give you the treasures of darkness,
riches stored in secret places,
so that you may know that I am the LORD,
the God of Israel, who summons you by name.

Isaiah 45:3

Then your light will break forth like the dawn,
and your healing will quickly appear;
then your righteousness will go before you,
and the glory of the LORD will be your rear guard.
Then you will call, and the LORD will answer;
you will cry for help, and he will say: Here am I.

Isaiah 58:8-9b

The LORD will guide you always;
he will satisfy your needs in a sun-scorched land
and will strengthen your frame.
You will be like a well-watered garden,
like a spring whose waters never fail.

Isaiah 58:11

The Spirit of the Sovereign LORD is on me,
because the LORD has anointed me
to preach good news to the poor.
He has sent me to bind up the brokenhearted,
to proclaim freedom for the captives
and release from darkness for the prisoners,
to proclaim the year of the LORD's favor
and the day of vengeance of our God,
to comfort all who mourn,
and provide for those who grieve in Zion—
to bestow on them a crown of beauty instead of ashes,
the oil of gladness instead of mourning,
and a garment of praise instead of a spirit of despair.
They will be called oaks of righteousness,
a planting of the LORD
for the display of his splendor.

Isaiah 61:1-3

I will give them a heart to know me, that I am the LORD.
They will be my people, and I will be their God,
for they will return to me with all their heart.

Jeremiah 24:7

The LORD is good,
a refuge in times of trouble.
He cares for those who trust in him.

Nahum 1:7

But Jesus immediately said to them:
"Take courage! It is I. Don't be afraid."

Matthew 14:27

Let us not become weary in doing good,
for at the proper time we will reap a harvest if we do not give up.

Galatians 6:9

Now to him who is able to do immeasurably more than all we ask or
imagine,
according to his power that is at work within us.

Ephesians 3:20

Finally, brothers,
whatever is true,
whatever is noble,
whatever is right,
whatever is pure,
whatever is lovely,
whatever is admirable—
if anything is excellent or praiseworthy—
think about such things.

Philippians 4:8

And as for you, brothers,
never tire of doing what is right.

2 Thessalonians 3:13

Cast all your anxiety on him because he cares for you.

1 Peter 5:7

This is the confidence we have in approaching God:
that if we ask anything according to his will, he hears us.

1 John 5:14

Printed in the United States
134724LV00003B/2/P

9 780982 044407